Patterns of Parish Leadership: Cost And Effectiveness In Four Denominations

Dean R. Hoge
Jackson W. Carroll
Francis K. Scheets, O.S.C.

Commentaries by
Most Rev. Thomas J. Murphy, D.D.
Dolores Leckey
Lyle E. Schaller
Loren B. Mead

Sheed & Ward

Sheed & Ward™ is a service of National Catholic Reporter Publishing Company, Inc.

Library of Congress Catalog Card Number: 88-61722

ISBN: 1-55612-208-X

Published by: Sheed & Ward
115 E. Armour Blvd. P.O. Box 419492
Kansas City, MO 64141-6492

To order, call: (800) 333-7373

Contents

Introduction

This book reports findings from a cross-denominational study of parish leadership, especially professionally trained leadership. Its focus is on several leadership options in use in these churches today, the costs of these options, and the perceptions of lay leaders about their effectiveness in meeting the needs of their parishes.

The four denominations in the study are the Roman Catholic Church, the Episcopal Church, the Lutheran Church in America (now part of the newly-formed American Evangelical Lutheran Church), and the United Methodist Church. We believe that these denominations have sufficient similarities that they can contribute to each other as each faces challenges of providing effective parish leadership in the years ahead. Their similarities include a shared tradition of emphasis on the sacraments—especially for Catholics, Episcopalians, and Lutherans—and an episcopal form of governance. Roman Catholic and Methodist bishops both have broad powers in matters of clergy deployment.

One additional similarity should be noted. Despite important continuing differences in the understanding of ministry, ordained and lay, these churches have converged a bit recently. The historic Protestant emphasis on the "priesthood of all believers" has led, at least in principle, to a view of ministry where clergy and laity share complementary roles and responsibilities. Although there have been major disputes in the Protestant denominations about the respective authority and responsibilities of clergy and laity, a basic belief in the calling of all Christians to share in ministry has persisted in all. This same affirmation is also at the heart of recent Catholic teachings

v

about ministry, especially since the Second Vatican Council. Traditional Catholicism had so elevated the role of the priest as being ontologically distinct from the laity that there was little role for laity in the church's ministry. But the Second Vatican Council affirmed that ministry belongs to all Christians and gave laity a participatory role in parish life. The Council also affirmed the ministry of laity in the world. Thus, although many Protestant-Catholic differences remain in the understanding of ministry, there has been an important convergence that makes comparative research valuable.[1] Catholics and Protestants can now learn from each other about their experiences with parish life.

As we noted, our focus is not on theological issues, but on the more mundane issues of costs of various forms of parish leadership and the attitudes of lay leaders towards them. We believe that as church leaders face hard decisions about options for parish leadership, they need the kind of information our study provides as well as an understanding of how the options agree with their theology of ministry and traditional practices. It is our experience that partisans for this or that option of parish leadership sometimes romanticize their idea while overlooking the practical issues of cost and effectiveness with laity. Thus our purpose is modest—merely to provide information about these issues in a cross-denominational perspective.

How the Study Came About

For several years each of the authors has been involved in the study of parish leadership. Two of us, Hoge and Scheets, have focused on leadership issues facing Roman Catholics. Hoge, a Presbyterian layman and sociologist at Catholic University, has been engaged in the study of vocations to the priesthood (Hoge, Potvin, and Ferry, 1984; Hoge, 1987) and a study of current

Catholic seminarians (Hemrick and Hoge, 1985; 1987). Scheets, a Catholic priest and church planning and management specialist, has directed two studies of the economics of Catholic theology schools (the CARA-Lilly study of 1980 and the NCEA update in 1985) and a major study of the future of center city parishes in Indianapolis, IN, Paterson, NJ, Perth Amboy, NJ, and Saginaw, MI (1981; 1987). Carroll, an ordained United Methodist minister and sociologist on the faculty of a Protestant seminary, has focused primarily on leadership issues facing Protestants, including a study of the supply and demand for clergy (Carroll and Wilson, 1980), a study of women clergy in Protestantism (Carroll, Hargrove and Lummis, 1983), and a study of seminary enrollment trends (Carroll and Roozen, 1984).

In various conversations, Hoge and Carroll agreed on the timeliness of new research gathering information on parish leadership across Protestant and Catholic lines. Some of the information needed by all denominations is very basic: What does it cost to have a full-time, ordained pastor, taking into account not only cash salary but also housing and a variety of fringe benefits and other indirect costs? What are the cost differences in the support of an unmarried priest and a married clergyman or woman? What are costs of providing clergy housing? What are the options open to parishes for leadership when there are no priests available or when the parish can no longer afford a full-time, resident, ordained pastor? How receptive are lay members to these various options? How do they judge the effectiveness of each?

A planning grant to Hartford Seminary from the Lilly Endowment, Inc., enabled Hoge and Carroll to develop a project to explore these issues. Early in the planning period, they invited several denominational officials and researchers to help shape the project. Father Scheets was one of the consultants, and Hoge and Carroll enlisted his assistance as a collaborator in the larger study. A second grant from the Lilly Endowment, Inc. made it possible for us to carry out the study during 1987. We describe the methods in Chapter 2.

Acknowledgements

Many people played important roles in the design and implementation of the project. We could not have proceeded without their help. Several national denominational officials helped pave the way for us by contacting bishops in the areas chosen for study. They include Most Rev. Thomas Murphy and Msgr. Colin MacDonald of the Roman Catholic Church, the Rev. Donald Treese of the United Methodist Church, the Rev. Joseph Wagner of the Lutheran Church in America, and the Rev. Preston Kelsey of the Episcopal Church. Regional denominational officials across the United States, too long a list to include here, helped by advising us in the selection of the parishes for study, encouraging them to participate, and providing information about the costs of professional leadership from judicatories. We also are indebted to the parish leaders, ordained and lay, who opened their parishes to our scrutiny: parish treasurers who provided financial information; pastors and lay officials who helped us with names and addresses of lay governing board members; and the governing board members themselves who filled out questionnaires. We are grateful for their help.

Besides this large group of people whom we cannot name here, we wish to thank several key persons. Helping us gather data in the eight regions were research coordinators who visited the parishes and denominational offices. They include: *New Hampshire area*, The Rev. Paul McHugh; Jean Mulligan; Marlene Eaton; The Rev. Forrest Laraba; *Texas area*, Patricia Storozuk; The Rev. Neale Jensen; Mary Avis; *Florida area*, Dennis A. Shearer; The Rev. Nicholas Godun; Carole Ross; *Alabama area*, Marsena A. Walsh; Paula M. Ross; Eleanor H. Weatherly;

New Jersey area, Susan Zahorsky; Teresa Stuhlmann; Patricia Reblitz; The Rev. Horace Frantz; *Ohio area,* Richard Krivanka; The Rev. Gay Jennings; Kathleen Slater; *Colorado area,* Jeri Thieme; Sue Brown; The Rev. William K. Christian, III; *Washington area,* The Rev. Linda Larsen; Ronald Lynch; John J. Kotalik, III.

Serving as consultants in the planning stage and at other times during the project were: The Rev. William Baumgaertner, Associate Director, Association of Theological Schools; David Grissmer, Ph.D., Research Economist, the Rand Corporation; The Rev. Preston Kelsey, Executive Director, Board for Theological Education of the Episcopal Church; Dolores Leckey, Executive Secretary, Bishops Committee on the Laity; Adair Lummis, Ph.D., Research Sociologist at Hartford Seminary; The Rev. G. Douglass Lewis, President, Wesley Theological Seminary; The Rev. Donald Treese, General Secretary of the Board for Ordained Ministry, United Methodist Church; and the Rev. Joseph Wagner, now Executive Director, Division for Ministry of the Evangelical Lutheran Church in America.

Ric and Joan Kriscka of RIC Corporation in Fort Wayne, IN, provided the software required for handling the financial data. Mary Jane Ross, Research Assistant at the Hartford Seminary, played a key role in managing the questionnaire process: supervising mailings, checking returns, supervising coding, and managing many complex processes with care and dispatch.

Finally, we are deeply grateful to the Lilly Endowment, Inc. for making the research possible. We especially appreciate the support given to us by Fred Hofheinz, Religion Program Director. Besides his important help in securing funding for the research, he gave us invaluable advice as we planned and carried out the study.

Organization of the Book

In Part One we discuss the major trends in parish leadership that lie behind the concerns of our research, and we describe the design and methods of our study.

Part Two (Chapters 3 and 4) contains a summary of the financial data. It depicts costs and remuneration for two types of parish leaders: ordained clergy and lay professionals.

In Part Three (Chapter 5) we turn to attitudes of lay leaders in the parishes. What do they believe about the desirability of the various options for parish leadership? How do they rate their current parish leaders?

Part Four includes a chapter (Chapter 6) giving our conclusions and reflections, then four commentaries written by leading experts in Catholic and Protestant parish life.

Throughout the book we have tried to avoid overwhelming the reader with statistics. Rather, we report our findings narratively with, we hope, a judicious selection of important tables and figures. More detailed statistics are given in the appendix.

Part One

Parish Leadership Today

1.
Parish Leadership: Trends and Issues

Catholics and Protestants today face difficult issues of ordained leadership. On the surface, the issues seem quite different, even mirror images of each other. For Catholics the core problem is a priest shortage which is already being felt in some parts of the country and which will grow dramatically by the end of the century. For mainline Protestants the problem is much different. Instead of a shortage of ordained clergy, many mainline denominations have a surplus or, at least, a "tight" situation in which finding positions for all available ordained clergy is difficult. At the same time, the mainline denominations have a growing number of small parishes that are unable to afford full-time ordained leadership and, in some instances, unable to attract any ordained leadership, either full-time or part-time.

These contrasting situations for Catholics and Protestants have a common result, and it is unwelcome: the assumption long taken for granted by most people that a parish will have a full-time, resident, ordained pastor is no longer possible for all. Each tradition must now discover new ways of deploying ordained clergy and meeting parish[1] leadership needs. In this chapter we begin an analysis of the problems and why they have arisen.

Changing Patterns of Leadership

Catholicism: Growing Membership, Shrinking Priesthood

Just how severe is the priest shortage facing the Roman Catholic Church in the United States? The most careful projections are those by Richard Schoenherr and Annemette Sorensen (1982). Also Dean Hoge has reviewed the priest shortage in his book *The Future of Catholic Leadership* (1987). We draw heavily on these studies.

Figure 1.1 reproduces Schoenherr and Sorensen's basic findings and shows dramatically the magnitude of the problem facing Catholics. The figure contains the actual trends for diocesan clergy through 1980 and three projected trends through 2000. The projections indicate a decline of approximately 40 percent in diocesan priests between 1980 and 2000. If the trend data also included priests who are members of religious orders, the decline would be even steeper. Several years have elapsed since Schoenherr and Sorensen made the projections, and today they have more information on what is actually happening.

They now believe that Projection B is the most accurate one (see Hoge, 1987:7).

Sharp as the priest decline is, it would be less critical if the membership of the Catholic Church were also declining. But this is not the case. Instead, Catholic membership has grown steadily during this century, exceeding the growth of the U.S. population through the mid-1960s and growing only slightly less than the population since that time. Thus today there is a grow-

Figure 1.1

Estimates of United States Active Diocesan Clergy Population, 1950-1975, and Projections, 1980-2000

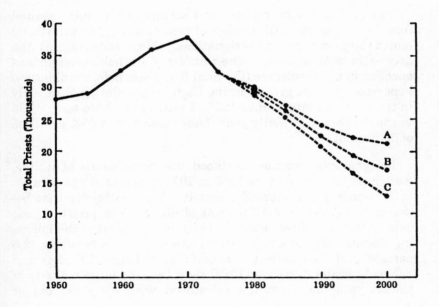

ing Catholic membership and a shrinking number of priests. This is clear when one looks at the rising ratios of members to priests. Figures from the *Official Catholic Directory*[2] indicate that there were 746 Catholics per priest in 1965. In 1975 the ratio was 827, and by 1985 it had grown to 912.

To put the Catholic situation in perspective we should note the corresponding ratios in the three Protestant denominations. In 1985, for the Episcopal Church, there were 196 members per clergy; for the Lutherans (LCA), there were 342; and for the Methodists, there were 247.[3] Furthermore, unlike the Catholic trend of a growing ratio of members per clergy, the ratios have shrunk in the three Protestant denominations. Thus the trends for Protestants and Catholics go in opposite directions. They are shown in Figure 1.2.

The decline in the number of Catholic priests has resulted from both a diminished number of men entering the priesthood and a large number of resignations. Most important is the decline in men entering. The number of Catholic seminarians enrolled in the theologate (the final four years before ordination) kept pace with the growth in the Catholic population from early in the current century until 1965. In that year there were 8,885 in the theologate. Twenty years later there were 4,053, a decline of 54 percent.

Resignations from the priesthood, the second source of decline, were greatest in the years 1966 to 1973, a period of upheaval in both church and the broader society. Hoge estimates that between 15 percent and 17 percent of all religious priests (those belonging to an order) active in 1970 resigned during the following decade. For diocesan priests the figure was between 12.5 percent and 13.5 percent. Studies by Greeley (1972:24) and Schoenherr and Sorensen (1982) show that the large majority of priests resigning from the priesthood were 45 years old or

Figure 1.2

**Members to Clergy Ratio, 1965-1985
Catholic, Episcopal, Lutheran, Methodist**

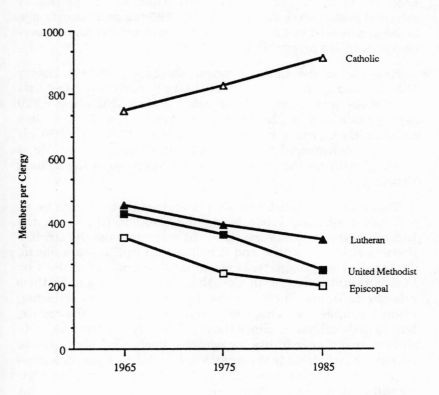

*Sources: Official Catholic Directory; United Methodist General
Minutes;* Yearbooks of American and Canadian Churches.

younger, and most often in their fifth to tenth year after ordination.

These two trends—declining entrants into the priesthood and numerous resignations by younger clergy—have had a further important impact. They have left Catholics with an aging priesthood. In 1970, 23 percent of diocesan priests and 29 percent of religious priests were over age 55. In 1985 the percent over age 55 had increased to 37 percent for diocesan priests and 56 percent of religious priests (Hoge, 1987:9).

How big is the Catholic priest shortage? Robert Sherry (1985), using an assumption that the 1975 parishioner-to-priest ratio of 791 was acceptable, estimated that in 1985 about 8,800 more priests were needed to reach the same ratio. By the same criterion the shortage will be approximately 13,000 in 1990. It must be remembered that the Catholic Church meanwhile is growing, with an expected growth of 10 percent in the coming decade.

This recital of statistics makes it obvious that to speak of an ordained leadership crisis facing the Catholic Church in the United States is no exaggeration. In some areas of the country there is already a crisis, and it will spread in the years ahead. The crisis, Hoge suggests, is not so much a crisis of faith (if by that is meant a decline in Catholics' faith in God and in their relation to Jesus Christ) as an institutional crisis reflecting Church policies regarding the priesthood, especially the restriction to male celibates. Since these policies do not seem likely to change in the near future, or perhaps at all, Catholics need to consider alternatives to the priesthood for meeting parish leadership needs. We will review some of them shortly. First, however, we will consider the Protestant situation.

Mainline Protestantism: Small Congregations and a Surplus of Clergy.

As we noted, the issues of professional leadership facing mainline Protestants seem almost mirror images of those facing Roman Catholics. Rather than a shortage of ordained clergy, mainline denominations have at least an adequate supply of clergy and in some cases a surplus. At the same time these denominations have a growing number of small parishes that are unable to afford full-time ordained leadership and, in some instances, unable to attract any ordained leadership, full- or part-time. Let us look at the available data from the three Protestant denominations in our study.

Unlike the Catholic Church, mainline Protestant church membership has declined substantially since the early 1960s. The declines were quite sharp for the decade from 1965 to 1975. The Episcopal Church lost 20 percent of its members; the Lutheran Church in America declined by 22 percent; and Methodists lost 11 percent (Carroll, Marty, and Johnson, 1979). Since that time the losses have abated somewhat; both Episcopalians and Lutherans had declines of 3 percent between 1975 and 1985, while the Methodists declined by 8 percent.

Meanwhile the number of ordained clergy increased. The increases between 1965 and 1985 ranged from 15 percent for the United Methodists to 21 percent for the LCA and 31 percent for the Episcopal Church.[4] The limited data available suggest that growth in active (non-retired) clergy may be levelling off slightly since the late 1970s; the number of ordinations has risen less rapidly than the number of retirements.

Earlier we looked at the ratio of members to clergy in several denominations. Let us look at the Protestant ratios once more in light of the trends in membership and clergy (see Figure 1.2). In 1965 there were approximately 350 Episcopal members per clergy. In 1975 there were 235, and by 1985 the ratio had shrunk to 196. For the Lutherans, the comparable ratios were 451 members per clergy in 1965, 389 in 1975, and 342 in 1985. For United Methodists, the ratios were 426 members per clergy in 1965,[5] 360 in 1975, and 247 in 1985. Thus while Catholic ratios were increasing dramatically, the Protestant ratios were decreasing.

The shrinking Protestant ratios have two related implications. The first is that, other things being equal, fewer members per clergy means that a larger proportion of overall contributions will go to clergy salaries and benefits. We are not able to say whether this has yet happened, since we lack trend data on total clergy costs. If it has not yet occurred, it is because, even with declining memberships, per-member contributions in the three Protestant denominations have increased. Figure 1.3 shows per-member giving trends (adjusted for inflation) for 1965, 1975, and 1985 for the three Protestant denominations and an estimate for Catholics for 1985. The increases are especially dramatic for Episcopalians (from $113 per member in 1965 to $178 in 1985—in 1967 dollars), but less so for Lutherans and Methodists.[6] Lutherans averaged $84 per member in 1965 and $95 in 1985. Methodists contributed $61 per member in 1965 and $77 in 1985. Comparable Catholic per-member giving (also adjusted for inflation) was $40 in 1985 (in 1967 dollars). The actual Catholic figure in current dollars, according to Hoge (1987:31), was about $125.

In spite of these increased contributions from a declining Protestant membership, we believe that our basic assumption is correct: a larger percentage of contributions will go to support clergy. Probably there is an upper limit to the increases in contributions that can be expected. As this limit is reached, there will be important questions of priorities in use of church resources; people will ask if such a high percentage of money going for leadership salaries is really warranted.

Figure 1.3

**Trends in Per Member Giving, 1965-1985
(Adjusted to 1967 Constant Dollars)**

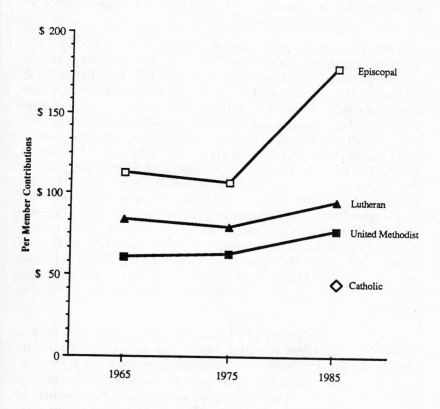

Sources: *Religion in America, 1950 to the Present;* Yearbooks of
American and Canadian Churches.

The second implication is that fewer members also mean shrinking parish sizes. In Figure 1.4, we compare the average size of congregations in the three Protestant denominations for 1975 and 1985. The average size of an Episcopal congregation dropped from 397 members in 1975 to 376 in 1985; Lutheran parishes went from an average of 518 members to 453 during the same decade; and United Methodist parishes dropped from an average of 255 members to 243.

These declines in parish size are not as sharp as the member-to-clergy ratios cited above in Figure 1.2, but they have important implications for the support of clergy. Lyle Schaller (1987:9) estimates that a congregation needs an average worship attendance of about 150 to be able to provide a meaningful workload and sufficient financial resources for a full-time resident minister. Schaller's rule of 150 worship attenders translates into a total membership of approximately 300. Some would no doubt argue that Schaller's figure is too high, and they would point to the numerous congregations with fewer than 150 active attenders who do have a full-time pastor. We agree, however, with the reasonableness of Schaller's figure as a general rule of thumb when both workload and resources are considered; it is a matter of the stewardship of resources, both of finances and leadership talent. Whatever the appropriate size for affording a full-time pastor, it is clear that a large proportion of Protestant congregations today are unable to meet Schaller's test, and the number is growing.

Studies by the Episcopal Church Clergy Deployment Office in the 1970s reflect this situation. They showed an increase in the number of vacant parishes at the same time that the denomination was experiencing an oversupply of clergy (Carroll and Wilson, 1980:39-40). This seeming anomaly was partly because of membership declines in many small parishes which in the past had been able to afford a full-time minister. As the result of both membership losses and the double-digit inflation of the late

Figure 1.4

Average Parish Size: Episcopal, Lutheran (LCA), and United Methodist Churches

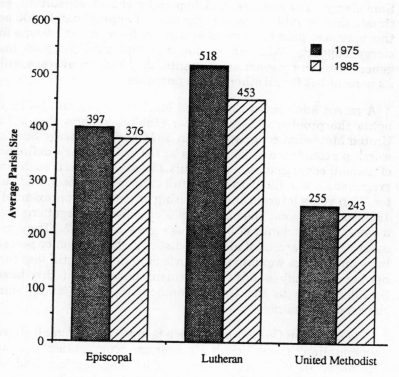

Source: Yearbooks of American and Canadian Churches.

1970s, they are no longer able to do so.[7] We do not have trend data on the size of congregations in the Episcopal Church, but a recent study (Roozen and Lummis, 1987) estimates that today 38 percent of Episcopal Churches have fewer than 100 communicant members, and 61 percent have fewer than 200. Another Episcopal study (Frensdorff and Wilson, 1987) agrees with Schaller's 150 attender lower limit for supporting a full-time clergy. The authors, a bishop and a church consultant, estimate that in 1985, Episcopal parishes of approximately 100 active members paid 65 percent or more of their parish income for clergy support. After these parishes also paid diocesan and general church program assessments, they had, on average, only 22 percent left for all other parish purposes.

A recent analysis in the United Methodist Church also highlights the problem. Lyle Schaller (1987:8) reports that 9,741 United Methodist congregations in 1974 had an average Sunday worship attendance of 35 persons or fewer (Schaller's definition of a small congregation). Given his 150 attender test, such congregations are unlikely to have a full-time resident ordained pastor. Ten years later, in spite of closing or merging approximately 1500 congregations, the number of Methodist congregations with a worship attendance of 35 or fewer grew to 10,127. They now constitute 27 percent of all Methodist churches. Seventy percent have an average worship attendance of under 100, still less than needed to justify a full-time resident pastor. On this basis, Schaller refers to the United Methodist Church as a "small church denomination."

The Lutheran Church in America is much less a "small church denomination" even though its average congregation size has decreased. In 1985 only 7 percent of its congregations had less than 50 attending worship on the average Sunday. Thirty-seven percent had an average worship attendance of under 100 persons. In number of members rather than worship attendance, 16 percent of Lutheran parishes had 150 or fewer members in 1985, and 34 percent had 250 or less.

Another problem in staffing small congregations is that many of them are located in small towns and rural areas, often a long distance from large population centers. In spite of the population movement out of metropolitan areas that has occurred since the early 1970s, many Protestant clergy do not want to serve small-town or rural parishes. Partly this is a result of working spouses, male or female, whose income is needed and whose employment opportunities are much better in metropolitan areas. Also single clergy, male or female, find it more difficult to establish friendships and support networks in small rural communities (Carroll, Hargrove and Lummis, 1982:168). These factors contribute to the mismatch between available jobs and clergy, exacerbating staffing problems in Protestant denominations.

The effect of membership declines is not limited to small congregations. Some larger parishes accustomed to multiple staffs have also lost enough members that they must reduce their staff or find other means to meet their leadership needs than full-time professional staff.

Different Types of Shortages

The issues of leadership facing Protestants are quite different from those facing Catholics. Both hold to the ideal of a full-time, resident, ordained pastor for a parish, and both face shortages that frustrate realizing this ideal. Catholics face a shortage of priests, and Protestants face a shortage of positions with finances adequate to support full-time clergy. Hoge outlines the possible types of "shortages" in church leadership:

The limitations to full-time church personnel in reality are (a) the number of candidates available for the positions, (b) the dollars available to pay them, and (c) the organizational structure available to coordinate and support them. The first is a supply factor; the latter two have to do with demand. If any of these limits are reached, we can speak of a "shortage," either of candidates, dollars, or organization. (1987:30-31)

For Catholics the shortage is one of candidates. There is no shortage of organizational support; the Catholic Church could readily absorb and deploy more priests were they available. Since Catholic giving is considerably less than Protestant giving (Greeley and McManus, 1987), there would seem to be potential for increased financial support under proper conditions. Whether at current levels of giving Catholics would be able to support a greater number of priests or, lacking additional priests, hire lay professionals, is a question we hope to help answer with our research. There is no shortage of lay professionals, but there is a widespread belief, as Hoge (1987:204) discovered, that the cost of replacing priests with lay professionals would be prohibitive. Is this the case?

For Protestants, as we have noted, there is no shortage of clergy. The most serious shortages are financial and organizational: there are not enough parishes able to support full-time ordained clergy adequately, not only financially but also of sufficient size to warrant a full-time resident pastor. Protestant denominations may not have reached their financial limits, but we suspect, as we noted above, that a shrinking membership will begin to push those limits severely.

We conclude, then, that if parishes are to have adequate leadership, both Protestants and Catholics must find alternatives to full-time, resident, ordained clergy. Already there are numerous options being discussed, and we look at them next.

Options for Parish Leadership

Possibilities for Catholics

In *The Future of Catholic Leadership*, Hoge analyzes eleven options open to Catholics for meeting the priest shortage. He classifies them under four major headings: Types A, B, C and D. It is instructive to list all eleven even though we are not concerned with all in this study. Here is the list:

Type A. Reduce the Need for Priests

1. Combine or restructure parishes, or re-educate Catholics to have lowered expectations for priestly services.

Type B: Get More Priests, with Existing Eligibility Criteria

2. Reassign or redistribute existing priests to get better utilization for parish leadership.

3. Get more parish priests from religious orders.

4. Get priests from foreign nations.

5. Recruit more seminarians.

Type C: Get More Priests, with Broadened Eligibility Criteria

6. Ordain married as well as celibate men.

7. Ordain women.

8. Institute a term of service for the priesthood, or institute an honorable discharge.

9. Utilize some resigned priests as sacramental ministers.

Type D: Expand the Diaconate and Lay Ministries

10. Expand and develop the permanent diaconate.
11. Expand and develop lay ministries. (pp. 86-87)

Hoge examines the pro's and con's of each of the eleven options and concludes that, short of a dramatic change in the number of candidates for the priesthood, the most likely options for the immediate future are numbers 10 and 11—an increase in the use of permanent deacons and professionally trained lay ministers to function as parish leaders under the supervision of a priest.

Let us look briefly at the diaconate option, even though it will turn out not to be of central concern to us—because our primary interest is in paid professional leadership, and the overwhelming majority of deacons are neither paid nor full-time.[8] The permanent diaconate, after centuries of disuse, was restored at the Second Vatican Council. Currently restricted to men (age 35 or older, married or single), deacons have a number of liturgical functions open to them in addition to carrying out acts of charity. They can administer baptism, reserve and distribute the Eucharist, preside over marriages, officiate at funerals, lead the worship of the people, and direct the liturgy of the Word. In these ways they can help relieve the shortage of priests. Yet there are several reasons why the diaconate is not a major option for relieving the priest shortage.

First, virtually all the deacons are part-time. A 1980 survey found that the average deacon devotes 13.7 hours per week to his ministry, which typically involves distributing Holy Communion, participating in liturgies, and visiting the sick and aged. Many priests complain that they need much more staff leadership carrying basic responsibility than deacons are able to give. As important as part-time and volunteer assistance is, institutions as complex as most Catholic parishes need full-time staff.

Second, the role of the deacon is unclear. Vatican II defined the diaconate theologically in terms of a status, but left the role or functions of a deacon to be negotiated in each work setting. This has led to considerable ambiguity, frustration and cynicism for both pastors and deacons. The pastors may be unaccustomed to sharing leadership or unskilled in delegating responsibilities, so the deacons often find themselves underemployed, except perhaps for assisting in the liturgy. Although this situation might be remedied by more adequate training of priests and deacons in staff relationships, it points to fundamental ambiguities about definition and identity.

Finally, there is opposition to the diaconate because it seems to strengthen both clericalism and male models of leadership in a time when laymen and laywomen are rediscovering their roles in the ministry of the whole people of God. There is little specific that the deacon can do that other laity, men and women, cannot do under the delegation of a bishop. As Joseph Komonchak (1985:23) observes, in many cases in the United States and elsewhere, "laymen and laywomen are undertaking ministries that are, in effect, indistinguishable from those for which deacons are ordained and include, as well, many of the functions for which priests are ordained." Why, then, critics ask, reestablish another vestige of clericalism, when the same functions can be carried out by laity? And why add to male-only models of leadership which the diaconate, as currently structured, mandates? Why not open leadership to all Christians who have the requisite dedication and training?

For at least these reasons, the permanent diaconate is unlikely to be a primary solution to the priest shortage. We are not arguing against the diaconate as an important vehicle within the total ministry of the Church. But we agree with critics that, as currently structured, it is not a primary answer to the priest shortage. If, however, there is clarification of the deacon's role, if more deacons are employed to work full-time, and if the diaconate is opened to all Catholics, then it will become an important option for meeting the Church's leadership needs. But those changes would make the diaconate little different from the development of lay professionals.

The use of lay professionals is a primary option for addressing the priest shortage. Lay professional ministers are very often full-time. They are frequently women religious (sisters), but they may also be married lay men or lay women who have professional training for particular ministry tasks.

Two Settings of Lay Professionals

The work of lay professionals occurs in two distinct settings. One of these, perhaps the most controversial, is in parishes where there is no resident priest, so-called "priestless parishes." They are growing in number. These are typically small parishes in villages or rural areas who discover that the bishop cannot any longer provide them with a priest. A study of Catholic parish life done at Notre Dame (Parish Project, 1982) estimated that in 1982, 4.5 percent of all Catholic parishes had no resident priest pastor. Another study conducted in 1985 for the National Pastoral Life Center (Elsesser, 1986), put the number of parishes without resident priests at 5.2 percent.

Many priestless parishes use lay professionals as "pastoral directors" or "resident ministers." These persons are most often women religious (as is the case in two parishes in our study). The lay professional lives in the parish. She or he is active in pastoral visitation, general parish administration, and committee meetings. She or he will preach and celebrate Communion[9] when the priest is not present. This pattern is controversial today. Among its most serious problems is the separation of sacramental ministry from the ongoing enabling ministry of the parish. The lay professional is with the people all week, constantly sharing in their lives and the life of the parish. The priest, however, who celebrates the sacraments, is in the parish only for a short time every week or two. Parishioners often do not get to know him well. As Hoge (1987:105) notes, "The psychological impact is to reduce the people's understanding of a sacrament to a kind of magic divorced from the human relationships which led up to it." There are also identity problems for lay professionals. Parishioners may not view them as "real" pastors, but only assistants. Gilmour (1986) reported that, in the case of women, they "remain second-class citizens in a church which is still male-dominated." And circuit-riding priests sometimes complain of the lack of opportunity to forge deep bonds with their parishioners. Gilmour believes that these problems make the use of lay professionals in priestless parishes a temporary rather than a permanent solution unless the status of the lay professional is clarified.

Not all priestless parishes meet their ministry needs with lay professionals as lay pastors. Some make use of a local lay person, designated as "pastoral leader" by a council of parishioners who are, in turn, appointed by the bishop. This lay person and council administer the parish under the supervision of a priest who visits the parish periodically and provides the sacraments.

The second setting for lay professionals is in a pastoral team in a parish or clusters of parishes along with one or more priests. In this setting there are none of the problems of the separation of sacramental from other pastoral ministries that we noted in priestless parishes. Rather, lay professionals function as parish administrators, religious educators, youth ministers, music directors, or other specialists within the parish. The use of lay professionals as part of a pastoral team working alongside one or more priests is clearly an option for large parishes, and lay professionals also may be used on pastoral teams serving small or mid-sized parishes. A report by the National Pastoral Life Center (1987) lists several options for combining priests and lay professionals in such parishes. These include linking (or "yoking" as Protestants have called it) two small or mid-sized parishes under the care of one priest, often supplementing his ministry with a lay professional; two or more parishes served by a pastoral team which includes priests (fewer in number than the number of parishes) working together with one or more lay professionals and/or deacons; and a parish cluster model, a variant of the previous model, where each parish retains its own priest but sponsors joint programs and activities with other parishes in the cluster. The joint programs are staffed by a team of lay professionals working together with the priests on a cluster team.

These options for using lay professionals to meet the priest shortage pose different challenges to Catholics, depending on whether they are viewed as temporary or permanent. As the Center report (1987:11) notes, if the options are viewed as temporary expedients until (and if) ordinations to the priesthood increase, then the primary concern of dioceses is to protect core values, such as the centrality of Eucharistic life, which may be endangered by some of the temporary adaptations. The centrality of the Eucharist is of concern to many Catholics profoundly disturbed by what they see as the substitution of Communion services presided over by lay professionals for the Eucharist celebrated by a priest (Broccolo, 1986). On the other hand, if the options to the traditional priesthood are viewed as more permanent, they represent a "transformation of ministry, and a realignment of the roles of clergy and laity." Such a transformation would have many implications.

We suspect that the options are not mere expedients, that at least some of them will be continued even if the priest shortage ends, and that, short of fundamental institutional changes in the priesthood, the shortage is not likely to end. Lay professionals are probably permanent.

Possibilities for Protestants

For Protestants, the options are no less difficult even though fundamentally different. Let us look at them from the standpoint of the three supply and demand variables noted above: persons, money and positions.

The adequate supply (or oversupply) of ordained clergy and the availability of positions (neglecting for the moment the issue of what constitutes a viable workload) would seem a happy situation were it not for the funds needed to support full-time clergy. There is a shortage of money. Since many small congregations cannot afford a full-time clergy salary, one strategy is for denominations to provide subsidies to enable these parishes to pay a full-time salary. Often the salary paid is some agreed-upon minimum established by the regional judicatory (diocese, synod, or conference). The congregation pays a portion of the salary, and the judicatory supplements the rest from funds which it receives from assessments on all the churches. A variant of this plan is for the congregation to apply to the judicatory for a grant to aid its ministry, a part of which is used to supplement the clergy's salary. Often the subsidy is used in combination with other options such as yoking or clustering, which we mention below.

There are several reasons, we believe, behind the growth of the minimum salary or subsidy option as a strategy for providing full-time ministry to small churches. We will mention three. One is a concern, especially in denominations that historically have emphasized a learned ministry, to make such a ministry available to as many congregations as possible. This is often very important as a mission strategy for new congregations or for older small congregations in areas of marked population growth. Second, offering a subsidy gives the denomination leverage to encourage or require some form of yoking or clustering to create an adequate workload for a full-time minister.

Third, it gives the denomination a way to deploy its ordained clergy, whom it has helped to educate at a considerable expense. This becomes a critical issue in times when there is a surplus of clergy, and it is especially important for a denomination such as the United Methodist Church which guarantees a pastoral appointment to all clergy who were ordained and accepted as full members of a conference. Simply put, if the denomination did not subsidize a large number of congregations (singly or yoked) who cannot afford the conference minimum salary, there would be a major crisis for those responsible for placing clergy.

In gathering data for this study, we did not investigate subsidies in any detail. But clearly there are both positive and negative aspects to subsidies. Not least among the latter is that denominational financial resources are limited, and their use for subsidies often conflicts with other priorities for ministry and mission.

Let us turn to the question of how to organize small congregations. Denominations have developed a number of options to serve the ministry needs of small congregations while also providing clergy with adequate salaries and meaningful workloads. These have been discussed by a variety of authors (e.g., Judy, 1973) and need only be listed here. They include:

Circuits or yoked fields: Two or more congregations of the same denomination (or sometimes of different denominations) are linked together to provide an adequate clergy salary. The congregations remain organizationally separate, though many activities may be undertaken cooperatively.

Consolidation and federation: Consolidation involves merging two or more small congregations of the same denomination into a single unit to create a viable ministry situation. Federation involves combining two or more congregations from different denominations into a single unit; the congregations retain their identification with their own denominations.

Extended ministry: A larger and financially strong church shares its ordained ministry with a nearby smaller congregation.

Clustering and group ministries: These patterns involve either a formal or voluntary linking of several congregations in a geographical area to work together to share resources (including leadership) and enhance programs. Generally a team ministry of clergy and lay professionals, fewer in number than the congregations in the cluster, share the leadership tasks. In addition to general pastoral oversight, the team is often able to provide specialized leadership in areas such as religious education, youth ministry or community outreach.

While these and other structural arrangements enable small congregations to have full-time professional leadership with adequate salaries and workloads, they have limitations. Mainly, they depend on getting congregations to enter cooperative relationships and put together sufficient financial resources (often subsidized by the denomination) to pay the salary of the clergy. This is often difficult. Therefore if the number of small churches continues to grow as a result of membership losses, and if salaries required for full-time clergy continue to increase, other options will be required.

This leads us to the existing alternatives to full-time ordained leadership. They are of two sorts: (a) use of ordained clergy who work part-time in a congregation and part-time or full-time in another job—either church-related or secular—and (b) use of various types of lay professionals.

Ordained clergy who are part-time in another occupation, church-related or secular, are referred to by various names: "tent-making" (after the Apostle Paul's support of his missionary activity by making tents), "bi-vocational," or "dual-role." Usually the clergyperson is compensated by both jobs, depending on the amount of time spent in each. But in some cases the full salary comes from the job outside the congregation, in which case he or she is called "non-stipendiary;" this pattern is often used in the Episcopal Church.

How widespread is this option? While we lack up-to-date figures, Bonn (1975) reported on several pertinent surveys conducted in the 1960s and early 1970s. His 1974 survey of clergy in nineteen Protestant denominations revealed that 22 percent of the clergy in these denominations supplemented their income as clergy with some form of secular employment. This represented an increase of four percentage points since 1968 and seven since 1964. Thirteen percent of all Protestant clergy in 1974 worked more than 20 hours per week in secular jobs. Bonn found that the lower the median salary paid in a denomination, the greater the number of clergy who worked more than 20 hours a week in the outside job. But the tent-making option was widespread even in denominations with high salaries—for example, in 1974, 19 percent of all clergy in the Episcopal Church (which had the highest median salary in Bonn's survey) were in some form of tent-making arrangement (Carroll and Wilson, 1980).

The pattern, long in use in many Protestant denominations, has the distinct advantage of providing trained professional leadership for small congregations (and sometimes specialized staff for larger congregations) at acceptable cost. Depending on the size of the congregation and the amount of time the clergyperson can give to the church, the tent-making pattern can be very satisfactory. Yet it has often been resisted by congregations, clergy, and denominations. For example, only recently did the United Methodist Church permit its ordained clergy (full conference members) to work less than full-time in a pastoral appointment, and even now it limits the number of consecutive years one can serve on a part-time basis.

The other option is the use of lay professionals, either full-time or part-time. The patterns in use are numerous, reflecting different assumptions about ordination and ministry. One pattern, not unlike the Catholic lay professional option, is to choose one or more lay persons from within a congregation who are then given special training and authorized to celebrate the sacraments and carry out other pastoral responsibilities *in that parish*. In certain cases they may be given a limited form of ordination. Some may also be permitted to serve in parishes other than their own. Most are part-time, but some work full-time. Finally, many lay professionals specialize in parish ministries other than preaching or sacramental leadership—for example, religious educators, youth ministers, parish administrators, music ministers, or parish visitors. It is our impression that such lay specialists are being used more and more as part-time staff in mid-sized and larger parishes in lieu of full-time ordained assistant ministers. The latter cost the parish more and frequently do not provide as much specialization as part-time lay professionals.

A final option, which would be highly controversial and thus unlikely, would be deliberate efforts to reduce the number of persons entering full-time ordained ministry. In times of clergy surpluses in the past, for example, during the 1930s Depression, there were calls for restricting the supply of clergy by tightly enforcing regulations for ordination (Carroll and Wilson, 1980:54). In the late 1970s, Episcopal bishops asked that Episcopal seminaries restrict admissions only to persons already under care of a diocese. This would allow the dioceses to anticipate the number of candidates for ordination. But it was not done. Seminaries have their own institutional needs which make them resist enrollment restrictions. Furthermore, they resist refusing admission to qualified persons who feel a calling to ministry. Therefore the denominational leaders will not be likely to reduce the supply of candidates except by one method—tightening standards for ordination. It is our impression that some of this has been happening recently.

We have spent some time describing the options for both Catholics and Protestants. There are similarities in the options and also important differences, reflecting different ecclesiological assumptions about ministry and opposite situations of clergy supply and demand. Both traditions are faced with hard choices. The various options we have noted have their partisan supporters who set forth theological and practical arguments. It is not our purpose in this book to examine the arguments; we merely try to provide data on the cost and perceived effectiveness of various options. We believe that Catholics and Protestants, in spite of different situations, have much to learn from each other in their efforts to provide good pastoral leadership for their people.

2.
Methods of the 1987 Research

Work began when we received a planning grant from the Lilly Endowment early in 1986. We recruited an Advisory Committee and called a meeting for May. The meeting covered many topics, including trends and upcoming problems in the various denominations, costs of parish life and seminary training, over-supply or under-supply of clergy, and problems of cooperation between clergy and lay leaders. Some persons recommended new detailed case studies of parishes or dioceses having innovative staffing patterns, others stressed research on whether higher staff salaries predicted more lay satisfaction with leadership, and yet others suggested studies of factors in financial giving.

We concluded that the most useful contribution would be a compilation of financial costs of professional parish staffs and collection of lay attitudes about them. This would aid church officials in estimating costs and effectiveness of various options for serving parishes unable to have a full-time clergy. For example, are full-time ministers with multiple parishes a better solution than part-time ministers in each parish, or even part-time lay leaders?

The Advisory Committee suggested a nationwide study, and it suggested four denominations—Catholic, Episcopal, Lutheran Church in America, and United Methodist. (The Lutheran Church in America later merged with other Lutheran denominations to form the American Evangelical Lutheran Church.)

27

Decisions About Financial Data Needed

In the summer months we interviewed denominational finance officers, and this helped clarify what kinds of financial data would be most needed. We set forth four goals. First was to ascertain the total "costs of doing business" to the parishes in having full-time ministers or priests, part-time ministers or priests, and lay professionals. That is, we wanted to add up cash salaries and all hidden costs to estimate the total financial burden for the parishes hiring these persons.

Second was to determine the costs of professional leadership support from the synod or diocese level and the national level. How much does the training, support and maintenance of the professional ranks cost the synod or diocese, beyond the funds expended at the parish level? And if costs are incurred at the national level, how much are they?

Third was to collect information on the remuneration of ordained clergy and lay professionals of various types, full-time and part-time. This was to help us compare their actual cash earnings.

Fourth was to calculate leadership costs per member. How much does professional staff cost per lay member or per household, and how many cents out of every dollar contributed go to pay for staff?

Other decisions were necessary too. We decided to limit our attention to actual expenditures, not budget amounts. We decided to include all part-time staff, ordained or non-ordained, so long as they were performing religious ministry and were being paid over $2000 a year; by including all these persons we could be more comprehensive in describing staff costs. Persons not in direct ministry (such as secretaries, bookkeepers or custodial staff) were not be to be studied, but we included directors of religious education, musical directors, youth ministers, liturgy directors, social service ministers and parish administrators. Finally, we excluded all costs of parochial schools attached to parishes.

It soon became clear that the most difficult task would be to estimate the costs of housing and feeding clergy who live in church premises, especially Catholic priests. The next chapter describes our approaches to the problem.

Francis Scheets collected report forms from past research and devised new forms for ordained clergy, lay ministers and Catholic sisters, plus a form for diocesan-level expenses. We pretested them in parishes of all four denominations and consulted diocesan finance officers in three denominations, then revised the forms. Scheets wrote a procedure book for the field staff, explaining all the definitions and giving instructions on recording the data.

Attitudinal Data

We discussed various ways of gathering attitudes about parish leadership effectiveness, and we decided on surveying the highest-level lay committees in each parish. In the Catholic parishes, these were the parish councils; in the Episcopal, the vestries; in the Lutheran, the church councils; and in the Methodist, the administrative boards. If there were 15 or fewer persons on any of these, we decided to give questionnaires to all of them; if there were more than 15, we randomly selected ten.

The questionnaire needed to be short and clear, focussing on feelings about the parish's leadership and on more general opinions about how parishes should be staffed. We drew up a first-draft questionnaire, pretested it in four parishes in the Washington, D.C. area, then revised it for final use. It was seven pages long. It did not ask for any names, but it requested written-in comments by the respondents on several topics. (It is included here in the appendix.)

Sampling Parishes

By late 1986 we knew that we could receive a second Lilly Endowment grant to carry out the total project, so we proceeded with designing the sample of parishes. Based on available resources we opted to survey eight regions in the nation and to gather data from 26 parishes in each—eight Catholic, six Episcopal, six Lutheran, and six United Methodist. The oversampling of Catholics was done because of the larger size of Catholic parishes (hence more complex finances) and the sparseness of past research on Catholic parish finances.

To select the eight regions we started with the nine U.S. census regions and combined the two adjoining regions having the lowest population (Mountain and West North Central), then randomly selected standard metropolitan areas in the eight. We randomly chose: Nashua, New Hampshire; Atlantic City, N.J.; Cleveland, Ohio; Colorado Springs, Colorado; Lakeland-Winter Haven, Florida; Mobile, Alabama; Longview-Marshall, Texas; and Bremerton, Washington. Since we expected the most difficulty getting permission from the Catholic bishops, we wrote to all eight immediately, and before long we received word from seven giving permission. One refused, and we substituted the adjoining diocese, whose bishop assented.

We were assisted in gaining cooperation from the Catholic bishops by Monsignor Colin MacDonald, Executive Director, Secretariat for Priestly Life and Ministry, National Conference of Catholic Bishops, and Most Rev. Thomas J. Murphy, Chair of the Bishops Committee on Priestly Life and Ministry. Archbishop Murphy contacted all the bishops, urging them to give permission for the study.

After the Catholic bishops assented, we contacted the Protestants. After a few hesitations here or there, all the bishops agreed to participate.

The goal of getting a defensible sample of U.S. regions was thus achieved, and the next problem was sampling parishes randomly within them. We decided to study three distinct types of parishes. *Type 1:* Parishes with more than one full-time clergy. Usually these parishes had additional part-time clergy and/or lay professionals, but these persons were not pertinent to the definition. *Type 2:* Parishes with one full-time clergy (possibly with part-time clergy or lay professionals in addition). *Type 3:* Parishes with less than one full-time clergy. These either shared a clergyperson with another parish, or had a part-time clergy or lay leader.

We thought it was necessary to compare the three types on costs and satisfaction. The distinction between Type 2 and Type 3 is central to the current discussion of options for clergy-less parishes. We decided on studying two parishes of each type in each region (a total of six) within each Protestant denomination and three of Type 1, three of Type 2, and two of Type 3 for Catholics (a total of eight).

Field Work

Data collection began in January 1987. We divided up responsibilities for the eight regions and travelled to each. The main task in each region was sampling parishes. Although we wanted to take a random sample within each of the three types, this was not feasible in all of the denominations because of lack of cooperation by some clergy. The problems seemed to be greatest among Catholic pastors, who were unaccustomed to financial research. Therefore we had to work with diocesan staff in each denomination to pick parishes known to be representative in terms of finances and staffing arrangements—and also possibly willing to participate. The diocesan staff therefore scanned the parish lists and reflected on which to pick: ("St. Marks in Smithville fits your needs exactly, but will Rev. Jones cooperate? I don't know.") We stressed that the parishes selected had to be a cross-section of the diocese or conference; we excluded unusual parishes (such as campus ministries or small ethnic groups) or parishes in the midst of leadership transition. We believe the selection of parishes was the best possible given our limitations, and although it is not a random sample in each region, it is representative enough to warrant cautious generalizations to the entire nation. The only obvious bias is that the parishes we studied tended to cooperate more than others with diocesan staff. Whether this affects the data we gathered is unknown.

We phoned the pastors of the parishes to discuss the research, and in most regions the diocesan staff also called. To the Catholic parishes we offered $100 for their help, and to the Protestants we offered $50. The Catholic figure was higher because the Catholic financial analysis was more time-consuming.

The second task was hiring local coordinators. We asked for recommendations from diocesan staff and hired three persons in each region to travel to the parishes and assemble the needed data. Most of the coordinators were financial staff from the diocesan offices, local parish treasurers, or members of parishes who were accountants. We scheduled training sessions in each region.

The third task in each region was to talk with financial officers of the dioceses and conferences to obtain diocesan-level information on expenditures for clergy support. These persons assembled the data from reports.

Later we returned to the eight regions for the training sessions. Then the coordinators travelled to the parishes and completed the tasks. Of the 208 parishes in the sample, they got complete data from 201. The other seven failed to follow through because of staff changes after our initial contact with them.

By mid-July all the data was in, and during the fall we carried out the analysis.

Part Two

Cost of Professional Parish Leadership

3.
Cost of Ordained Clergy

This chapter and the next are devoted to the analysis of costs of professional leaders in parishes. They summarize the practices we found in the four denominations as of 1986. Chapter 3 is on full-time and part-time clergy costs, and Chapter 4 is on lay ministers.

Available Information for Ordained Clergy

The present study continues a tradition of clergy cost research which is decades old. Here we will mention a few recent studies which were helpful to us in designing the new research. An important survey of 19 Protestant denominations was done by Robert L. Bonn in 1973, published with the title *Clergy Support Study* (Bonn, 1974). It did a thorough job in adding up cash salaries and numerous benefits to estimate the total cost of clergy to parishes. A recent study was done by the National Association of Church Business Administrators (NACBA) and published in 1986 (NACBA-MSFA, 1986). Its data are unfortunately based on a low return rate to a questionnaire survey, hence not reliable; only 962 parishes responded to the survey out of 24,000 to whom questionnaires were sent. We mention this survey but will not refer to its findings.

Whereas Protestant clergy salaries are fairly well known because of annual yearbook reports and periodic surveys, this is not true for Catholic priests. A thorough nationwide study of costs of priests has never been done. The best Catholic data known to us come from a 1975 task force set up by the Diocese of Richmond (Virginia) to study salaries, stipends and benefits. This study found the total cost of priests to average $13,700 at that time. In 1988 dollars this would amount to about $29,700.

Several other studies have been done on specific aspects of cost or compensation of priests (e.g., Diocese of Pittsburgh, 1978). In 1977 the National Federation of Priests' Councils gathered data on cash income of priests, and in 1984 they updated it, resulting in a booklet *The Laborer is Worthy of His Hire* (NFPC, 1984). The 1984 survey included an estimate of "all fringe benefits, except room and board." But room and board is a crippling exclusion. In addition detailed information was not supplied by many dioceses, reducing the report's value. Lastly, the National Association of Treasurers of Religious Institutes conducted a detailed survey of compensation provided to Catholic religious men and women in 1985 and 1987 (NATRI, 1985; 1987). As with the NFPC survey, detailed data on allowances, benefits, and housing were lacking.

Information Collected on Clergy Costs

Existing studies have weaknesses which limit their usefulness. In none of them were Catholics and Protestants studied in parallel to permit comparison. Also most existing Catholic studies lacked comprehensive estimates of total costs of supporting clergy; they were usually too vague in the areas of allowances and benefits to be of much use. Therefore in the new study we set out to get maximally reliable information on the *total cost of professional ministers* to the local parish and also to the supporting diocese, synod or conference.

It seems useful here at the outset to describe the information we gathered and the procedures we used, so the reader can more quickly grasp the findings. The main complexities occurred with respect to salary, housing and professional allowances. We take up each in turn.

Salary

We gathered information only on the actual income of the clergy from the parish and/or other religious employment. We paid no attention to other income of the clergypersons, either from non-religious part-time work or from other sources such as investments or estates. We wanted actual data from the most recent year for which there were records (usually 1986) in the following categories:

1. *Base Salary:* The contract dollar salary paid by the parish.

2. *Ministry Supplement:* Income received from another (yoked) parish, from the supporting diocese, synod or conference, or from parish sources (e.g., authority to take a

percentage or dollar amount from a particular Sunday collection). We specifically included payments by the parish for retirement or pension, medical or health insurance, social security and anything else (e.g., Workmen's Compensation Insurance or life insurance). For clergy performing religious duties for the diocese or synod, their salary for those duties was included.

3. *Other Ministry-Related:* Income received for ministerial or sacramental services (e.g., honoraria, stipends or stole fees). These are received from individuals, not the parish treasury, yet they can be considered normal professional income. We asked each clergyperson to report on the total in the previous year.

Housing

The estimation of total costs to the parish of housing clergy was difficult. From past research we expected it would be the trickiest task in the whole project. The problem was not bad for clergy owning or renting their own homes, since they typically receive housing allowances and pay all their own housing costs. (In the parishes studied here, over ninety percent of Lutheran ministers, over eighty percent of Episcopals and about half of Methodists owned their own houses.) But the problem was complicated for clergy in parish-provided housing—about half of the Methodist clergy and almost all of the Catholic priests. We gathered data as follows:

Housing Operations Cost: For clergy who owned or rented their homes, the figure is the amount received each year.[1] When housing is provided for the clergy, we needed to estimate the institutional costs of doing so. In parishes where clergy housing expenses are mixed in with other parish plant expenditures, we were faced with the task of allocating these costs (including plant maintenance and housekeeping) of the rectory, based on the percent of total parish plant square footage in the rectory and the total utilities and maintenance costs for the parish. We did not try to gather any costs associated with capital expenditures such as depreciation, mortgage, and interest payments. Estimating rectory costs was relatively straightforward when the rectory was used solely for housing the parish clergy (normally the case with Protestant clergy). Then we merely allocated costs based on a percentage of total square footage of the parish property.

In allocating actual housing costs for Catholic priests, we used a two-stage procedure. First we determined the approximate square footage of each building covered by parish plant maintenance and operation expenses, and then we determined the share of these costs to be assigned to the rectory, based on the percent of total parish plant square footage represented by the rectory.

But Catholic rectories are often multi-purpose buildings, including offices and meeting rooms, and also in many cases they were built to provide housing for more clergy than are presently living in them. To determine the space actually occupied by the clergy for their living, we employed the concept of "Net Assignable Square Footage" (NASF), which Scheets had found useful in a study of Catholic seminaries (1985).[2] NASF is defined as the interior square footage of a building actually being used for a definable purpose. It excludes hallways, storage space, and so on. We had to employ two definitions of NASF: the first was strictly for personal clergy use, with the rest of the rectory floor space being assigned for parish life. To get this NASF we had to obtain the interior square footage required by clergy for personal use: bedroom, study, dining room (if used), and kitchen. If several parish clergy lived in the rectory, the square footage of their common rooms was divided equally. The resulting figure was used when obtaining a reasonable rental value from a knowledgeable realtor.

The second NASF included, in addition to clergy living space, the extra living quarters, offices, and meeting rooms in the rectory. Unused rectory space was not included. The ratio of the first NASF to the second was used to calculate a reasonable percent of actual rectory plant costs required by parish clergy.

The percentage of rectory costs represented by unused rooms, offices, and meeting rooms, was considered to be a cost to the parish but not a cost of housing clergy. Thus the Catholic priests living in mammoth rectories built for a different age were not "penalized" in our cost calculations, since they received no benefit from the excess space. The cost of maintaining unused space cannot in justice be included in the expense of housing clergy.

Comparable Rental Value: This was an estimated rental value of the living space occupied by the clergy of the parish. We used the NASF and conferred with a local realtor to arrive at a realistic figure, which was then used in all of our housing cost calculations.

Utilities: Many parishes provide their clergy with a utility allowance, and if so, it was included in the cost figures.

Other: Any other costs associated with clergy housing, paid by the parish, were included.

Food: Costs of food were estimated in parishes where clergy ate in the rectory or parish dining room. Then the total food costs (including a cook's wages, if any) were allocated to each person or category of persons who ate there. To do this we got estimates of the number of meals eaten by each clergy and any other persons eating there regularly. The proportion of total meals eaten by any clergy determined the estimate of the cost of feeding him. (It should be noted that the procedures we followed in allocating housing and food costs are those generally accepted by accountants in determining unit costs.)

Professional Allowances

We gathered actual expenditures by the parish for all professional allowances. They included (1) *transportation*, that is, any allowances for car or other transportation costs; (2) *education*—actual expenditures incurred for meetings, books and journals, and continuing education; (3) other allowances.

Information on Parish, Staff, and Contributions

We requested data on the number of baptized members and the number of households in the parish. Catholic parishes are typically described in terms of number of households. Protestant parishes are described in number of members, but some include infants in their membership lists while others do not; for sake of uniformity we used the total number of baptized members for each parish.

We also requested the amount each parish received as total collections (apart from school contributions if the parish has a school) and their total ordinary operational expenditures (excluding capital expenses and school subsidy). The relationship of these two figures indicates the ability of each parish to support its ordinary programs with its collections—or its need to cover program costs by other means of fund-raising.

Table 3.1 indicates average parish sizes and laity-to-clergy ratios. The first column has average size of parishes in our study. The average Catholic parish we studied had a membership of nearly 3,350. The average Episcopal parish had 476,

Table 3.1 Average Parish Sizes and Laity Per Staff Ratios

	Average Parish Membership		Laity per Full-Time Clergy	Laity per Full-Time Staff (Clergy + Lay)
	in Sample	in Nation		
National Average:				
Catholic	3,348	2,706	1,954	1,064
Episcopalian	476	376	313	226
Lutheran	411	453	304	249
Methodist	703	243	398	356

Source: Appendix A.1 and A.3

Lutheran parish 411, and Methodist parish 703. These parishes are larger than the actual national average for each denomination because of our decision to sample particular types of parishes.

The second column shows nationwide average parish sizes in the four denominations; the figures were found by dividing total membership as reported in yearbooks by the total number of parishes. Comparison of the first two columns demonstrates the amount of bias in our sample.

In all four denominations, parishes with two or more full-time clergy were somewhat larger—the average Catholic parish had 5,349, the Episcopalian 822, the Lutheran 734, and the Methodist 1,757. (See appendix Table A.2.) One-clergy parishes were smaller—the Catholic averaged 2,272, Episcopal 376, Lutheran 352, and Methodist 313. Parishes without full-time clergy were much smaller—the Catholic averaged 634, Episcopal 76, Lutheran 91, and Methodist 159.

Table 3.1 also shows ratios of members to clergy in each parish, as a rough indicator of workload. We found the average Catholic priest responsible for about 1,950 members, while the clergy in the Protestant parishes averaged being responsible for a little over 300. When parishes had two or more clergy, the Catholic ratio of clergy to members jumped to 2,149, the Episcopal and Lutheran ratios jumped to a little over 380, and the Methodist ratio jumped to 604. When we look at ratios of members to total full-time staff (clergy and lay), again we see much higher figures for Catholic parishes than Protestant parishes (Table 3.1, last column). The ratios are shown in Figure 3.1.

Faced with such large ratios of people to clergy, it is no wonder that the Catholic parishes have been employing more and more professional lay ministers. We found numerous full-time lay professionals in the Catholic parishes studied, and 77

Figure 3.1

Members Per Full-Time Staff, Ordained and Lay, in Parishes with Different Numbers of Clergy

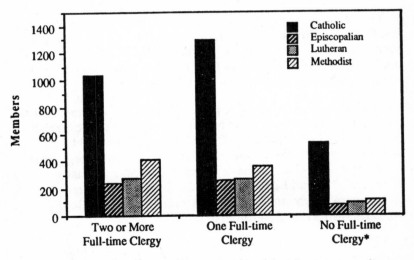

*No full-time clergy in the parish. There is either a part-time clergy or one serving more than one parish. In the latter case the number of members in the figure is for the parish in our sample.

percent of them were in parishes with two or more priests. The impact of full-time lay professionals on member-to-staff ratios is greatest in the Catholic parishes (a drop from 1,954 to 1,064), but the ratio is still over four times as large as it is for Protestants.

Three more statistics describing the parishes are shown in Table 3.2. First is the average contribution per household, which was $278 for Catholic parishes, $599 for Episcopal, $653 for Lutheran, and $553 for Methodist. We looked at differences in parishes having different levels of clergy staffing, and we found that in general the contributions per household are higher in small parishes without full-time clergy. (See appendix Table A.4.) Our data agree with the 1986 report, *The Charitable Behavior of Americans,* sponsored by Independent Sector (Yankelovich, 1986) and with Hoge's analysis in *The Future of Catholic Leadership* (1987); Catholics are lower in church contributions than Protestants, even though levels of family income are similar. Hoge reported that in 1982-84, approximate median family income for American Catholics was $20,500, for Episcopalians it was $25,300, for Lutherans $20,500, and for

Table 3.2 Contributions Per Household and Relation of Expenses to Contributions

	Contribution Per Household	Expenses as % of Contributions	Salaries as % of Expenses*
National Average:			
Catholic	$278	100%	31%
Episcopalian	599	107	48
Lutheran	653	99	51
Methodist	553	98	38

Source: Appendix A.4

* Salaries include all full-time and part-time professional staff, ordained and non-ordained.

Methodists $18,300. Yet Catholic contributions were much lower. (Also see Gallup and Castelli, 1987.)

The second column in Table 3.2 is the ratio of parish expenses to contributions. The averages for all four denominations are close to 100. The Episcopalian parishes are the most dependent on outside fund-raising for balancing their budgets. The last column in the table indicates that Catholic and Methodist staff salaries absorbed about one-third of ordinary expenses (31 percent and 38 percent). Episcopalian and Lutheran parish staffs required about one-half of the ordinary parish expenses (48 percent and 51 percent). These figures are correlated with member-to-staff ratios in Table 3.1—the more members per staff, the lower percent of expenses go for staff salaries. In all four denominations the figures are also associated with parish size, in that the smaller the parish (on average) the higher the percentage of income is devoted to staff salaries. (For related Protestant data see Hartley, 1984.)

Table 3.3 presents the estimated breakdown of parishes in each denomination according to their staffing patterns. These figures were not taken from our 1987 research, since our method of sampling parishes precluded it. We needed the information, so we consulted with officials in the four denominations to get their best information (or even their best guess) about the reality. The figures are estimates only, since little reliable information exists. For example, an estimated 50 percent of Catholic parishes in the late 1980s had two or more full-time priests, 45 percent had one priest, and five percent had less than a full-time priest (see Elsesser, 1986). These figures were used in computing the overall statistics we report for each denomination. Since our sampling method produced an overrepresentation of large parishes, we had to adjust all the statistics to make them more representative of *all* parishes.[3] This was done for all the dollar figures for clergy in the present report.

Table 3.3 Estimated Percent of Parishes by Staffing
Pattern by Denomination

| | Ordained Clergy | | |
	Two or More	One	None Full-Time
Catholic	50%	45%	5%
Episcopalian	18	54	28
Lutheran	36	44	20
Methodist	16	39	45

Average Total Compensation for Ordained Clergy

Total compensation for full-time ordained clergy is summarized in Table 3.4 and Figure 3.2, adjusted for staffing patterns. The average for Catholic clergy was $26,184; for Episcopal clergy it was $41,029, for Lutheran clergy $39,059, and for Methodist clergy $35,308.[4] The Catholic figure is far lower than the others. This surprised us, since we expected the four figures to be more similar to each other.

The differences among the Protestant clergy are not due to dollar income disparities, since the figures are much the same (third column in the table). Rather, the differences result from levels of housing and other benefits, where the Episcopalian clergy receive considerably more. Episcopalian housing and benefits add up to $19,268, compared with $17,371 for Lutherans and $14,475 for Methodists. The Catholic versus Protestant difference is almost entirely in the lower dollar income received by Catholic priests; housing and other benefits are similar. The Catholic priests reported an average dollar income of only $7,472. The figures in the second column of Table 3.4 represent

Table 3.4 National Adjusted Average Total Compensation for Full-Time Ordained Clergy (Sample Parishes: 1986 Fiscal Year)

	Number of Clergy	Total Compensation =	Dollar Income +	Housing & All Benefits
Catholic	98	$26,184	$ 7,472	$18,712
Episcopalian	58	41,029	21,761	19,268
Lutheran	51	39,059	21,688	17,371
Methodist	59	35,308	20,833	14,475

Source: Appendix A.5

Figure 3.2

Average Total Compensation of Full-time Clergy (Adjusted Data)

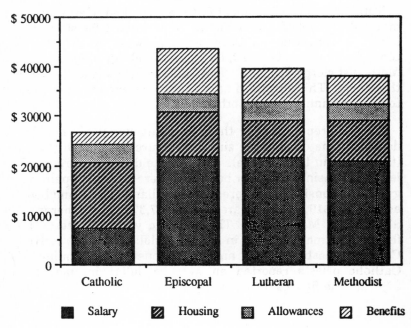

our best estimate of total costs, at the parish level, of employing full-time clergy.

Economic conditions vary by region, so we distinguished three major regions in our data—the Northeast (New Hampshire, New Jersey and Ohio), the Southeast (Florida, Alabama and Texas), and the West (Colorado and Washington). Table 3.5 and Figure 3.3 portray the information for each region.

For Catholic clergy there is a difference of nearly 32 percent in total compensation from region to region, with those in the West receiving the most and those in the Southeast the least. The dif-

Table 3.5 Regional Adjusted Average Total Compensation for Full-Time Ordained Clergy

	Number of Clergy	Total Compensation	=	Dollar Income	+	Housing & All Benefits
Roman Catholics:						
Northeast	37	$26,070		$7,745		$18,325
Southeast	42	23,681		6,012		17,669
West	19	30,662		10,109		20,553
Episcopalians:						
Northeast	19	$46,501		$20,739		$25,726
Southeast	23	40,424		24,440		15,984
West	16	40,524		20,341		20,183
Lutherans:						
Northeast	20	$35,534		$18,388		$17,146
Southeast	19	27,051		14,490		12,561
West	12	38,055		20,247		17,808
Methodists:						
Northeast	19	$20,965		$12,014		$8,951
Southeast	18	20,844		11,099		9,745
West	22	35,790		21,909		13,881

Source: Appendix A.5

Figure 3.3

Average Total Compensation of Full-time Clergy

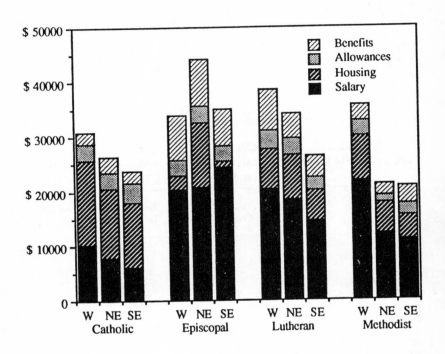

ferences occur both in dollar income and in housing allowances and benefits; in both categories the West is clearly the highest.

For Episcopal clergy the regional differences are small. But for Lutheran and Methodist clergy they are fairly large; the Lutheran clergy in the West received about 40 percent more in total compensation than those in the Southeast. Probably this is due in part to the smaller sizes of Lutheran churches in the

Southeast. Finally, the Methodist clergy in the West receive substantially higher compensation than those elsewhere—72 percent more. The difference is largely in dollar income, which is $21,909 in the West, compared with $12,014 in the Northeast and $11,099 in the Southeast.

Housing Costs

Housing costs for clergy are handled in very diverse ways. In years past the local parish was typically expected to provide housing for the pastor, but in recent decades more and more clergy, especially Episcopalian and Lutheran, have preferred to own their own homes. Today many parishes give such clergy a housing allowance rather than a parsonage; the allowance is not subject to income tax if kept within government regulations. The Methodist system of deploying clergy does not allow as much flexibility as other Protestant systems regarding clergy owning their homes.

In our study, for parishes which provided a rectory or parsonage, we used the fair rental value of the space, based on the usable square footage. For Catholic clergy (as explained above) we estimated the rental value for only the net assignable square footage of the space used for personal living. Look at Table 3.6. It provides information on the average allowances *for those receiving such allowances;* others are not represented in the table. The first column is the total housing allowance received. (Social Security taxes, but not income taxes, are paid on housing and utilities allowances.)

The second column shows the allowances granted to clergy living in parish-provided housing. For Catholic priests this covers food and some utilities; for Protestants it is understood to cover utilities.

Table 3.6 Adjusted Average Housing Allowance for Full-Time Clergy: Showing Denominational Cost for Utilities & Food, and Rent*

| | Clergy Who Own or Rent Home | Parish-Provided Housing | |
		Housing Allowance	Comparable Rental Value
Catholic		$8,536	$ 4,763
Episcopalian	$10,922	4,284	11,367
Lutheran	9,175	2,509	9,550
Methodist	9,956	3,828	7,778

*For those receiving housing allowances or furnished housing. Source: Special analysis of Appendix A.5 & A.6

The third column reports the fair rental value of the parish-owned housing, as estimated by a realtor. For the Catholics the estimate is for a comparable apartment off parish premises. The fair rental value can be understood to include the true costs of owning property, including taxes, depreciation and normal capital improvement needs.

The majority of Protestant clergy live in their own homes and they receive a housing and utility allowance from the parish. Of the clergy living in parish-provided quarters, the Episcopalians have the highest quality housing among the Protestants (judging from rental values), while the Catholic priests' quarters are relatively modest. These rental values are not out of line with national averages today. A 1987 study by the U.S. League of Saving Institutions estimated that the median monthly housing expense in the U.S. was $722, or $8,664 per year (*Wall Street Journal,* 1988). The monthly figure included $601 for mortgage and $121 for taxes and hazard insurance.

To exemplify the diverse practices today, by far, most Catholic priests live in rectories; only one in our study did not. Ninety percent of the Episcopalians and Methodists received an allowance for housing and/or utilities, and 88 percent of the Lutherans did so. Nineteen percent of the Episcopalian clergy and 8 percent of the Lutheran clergy lived in parish-provided housing, but for Methodists the figure was 44 percent.

We looked at parishes with two or more ordained clergy, compared with those with one clergy, and we found no differences in housing costs. But clergy less than full-time in any parish (usually serving more than one parish or doing other religious work) received much less housing benefit from any single parish.

Allowances for Travel and Education

Table 3.7 includes monies paid by the parish for travel, books, journals, membership in organizations, conferences and training workshops. The figures in the table are for clergy receiving such allowances—in the case of travel, 85 percent of the Catholics, 74 percent of the Episcopalians, 92 percent of the Lutherans, and 78 percent of the Methodists; in the case of education, all of the Catholics, 72 percent of the Episcopalians, 84 percent of the Lutherans, and 68 percent of the Methodists. The payments for travel varied little from denomination to denomination; the overall average was about $2,970. For education the payments varied from a high of $598 for Episcopalians to a low of $473 for Methodists. (Additional payments for continuing education of

Table 3.7 Adjusted Average Travel & Education Allowances for Full-Time Clergy Receiving Allowances

	Travel	Education
Catholic	$3,121	$531
Episcopalian	2,932	598
Lutheran	3,000	544
Methodist	2,822	473

Source: Appendix A.5

clergy from the diocese, synod, or conference are discussed below.)

Regional variations in travel and education allowances are complex, but in general the allowances are higher in the Western states than elsewhere. (See appendix Table A.5 for details.)

Retirement and Health Benefits

Before we get into this topic, we should clarify the situation regarding social security. By federal law clergy are considered self-employed, and they generally pay their own social security payments (based on the Self Employment Contribution Act, or SECA). When we gathered the data for this study we included the usual retirement and health benefits, and we also included social security payments and "other" benefits—occasionally workmen's compensation and life insurance. The availability of these last two benefits varies. Forty-seven percent of Lutheran clergy received social security or other benefits, whereas only 8 percent of the Methodist clergy received social security and 5 percent "other" benefits. Thirty-six percent of the Episcopalian clergy had part or all of their social security paid by the parish, and 29 percent received "other" benefits. Only 17 percent of the Catholic priests received either of these two. (See appendix Table A.6.)

Except for Catholic clergy, the amounts were significant. Of the clergy receiving these benefits, the average Episcopalian clergy received $2,394, the average Lutheran $1,872, and the average Methodist $1,274. The Catholic figure was lower—$405.

Table 3.8 shows the adjusted national average retirement and health benefits received at the parish level by full-time clergy. For retirement the Episcopalian clergy received the most, $4,609. The Lutheran and Methodist clergy received slightly over $3,000, and the Catholic priests received the least, $999.

Table 3.8 Adjusted Average Retirement & Health Benefits for Full-Time Clergy

	Retirement & Other	Health	SECA*
Catholic	$ 999	$1,381	$ 399
Episcopalian	4,609	2,824	1799
Lutheran	3,229	1,649	1872
Methodist	3,018	1,444	1274

Source: Appendix A.5
*Social security and workmen's compensation (if paid).

(Sizable contributions to clergy retirement are also made at the diocesan, synod and conference level. We discuss them below.)

For health care, average parish payments for Catholic clergy were $1,381 and for Episcopalians they were $2,824. For Lutherans they averaged $1,649, and for Methodists, $1,444.

(As with retirement benefits, there were contributions for health care from the diocesan, synod, and conference levels.) Social security payments by the parish varied widely, as did the percentage receiving them—17 percent of the Catholics, 36 percent of the Episcopalians, 47 percent of the Lutherans, and 8 percent of the Methodists.

We found only small differences in the payments by parishes for retirement and health benefits between multi-clergy parishes and single-clergy parishes. But for clergy serving more than one parish or working part-time outside the parish, the payments are much lower. We looked also at regional variations. Catholic clergy in the Northeast received higher retirement benefits than others, but not higher health benefits. Episcopalian clergy in the Southeast and West received higher retirement and health benefits than those in the Northeast. Lutheran clergy in the

West had higher benefits than others. And Methodists in the West had higher health benefits (but not retirement benefits) than others. (See appendix Table A.5.)

Average Clergy Cost Per Household

How much does an average Catholic, or Lutheran, household in a parish pay for its clergy? This is important to know in any discussion of parish leadership cost and effectiveness. Recall that parishes vary widely in size from denomination to denomination. As Table 3.1 showed, the Catholic parishes in our sample averaged 3,348 members while the Protestant parishes averaged 530. In short, the Catholic parishes were over five times as large. (The size difference is even greater if we look at *all* Catholic parishes in the U.S. compared with *all* Protestant parishes.)

In our sample the total compensation of each ordained clergy per household was $40 in the Catholic Church, $241 in the Episcopal Church, $382 in the Lutheran Church in America, and $282 in the United Methodist Church. These figures varied greatly *within* each denomination, depending on the number of clergy in the parish. Parishes without a full-time pastor had to pay much more per household for their leadership. In those parishes—normally very small—the clergy cost per household was $141 for Catholics, $852 for Lutherans, and $422 for Methodists. For Episcopalians the data was erratic, but the figure was high. In parishes with one clergy, the Catholic cost per household was $41, the Episcopal cost was $216, the Lutheran cost was $293, and the Methodist cost was $176. In parishes with two or more full-time clergy the figures were $37 for the Catholics, $255 for the Episcopalians, $229 for the Lutherans, and $148 for the Methodists.

Again we see that Catholic parishes are quite different from Protestant parishes. Their cost of operation per member is much lower. American Catholics pay much less per member for their religious leadership.

Average Support of Clergy by Dioceses, Synods, or Conferences

In undertaking our study of the "true economic costs" of full-time ordained clergy, we realized that some costs are not paid directly from parishes. Certain program costs are directly sponsored by the diocese, synod, or conference—albeit the funds for these programs come from parish assessments. We made a serious attempt to get cost figures of all such programs. In doing so we needed to make numerous judgments about how to allocate program costs, and we decided to include only *program* costs borne by the diocese, synod, or conference, not any salary or office costs. For example, we gathered cost data on continuing education seminars for clergy, but not on salary figures of diocesan or synod staff responsible for sponsoring such seminars. This was done for sake of clarity and comparability. We broke down the judicatory costs into five categories, which we will discuss under two headings: personal and career assistance; insurance, retirement, and other.

Personal and Career Assistance

Table 3.9 shows judicatory costs per active clergy for personal and career assistance. Personal assistance includes both personal counseling and continuing education, and career assistance includes career counseling, moving and deployment, and spouse assistance programs. The Catholic dioceses spent the largest sums for personal counseling and continuing education

Table 3.9 Support Programs by Diocese, Synod, or
Conference Per Active Clergy: Personal and Career
Assistance

	Personal Assistance		Career Assistance
	Personal Counseling	Continuing Education	
Catholic	$290	$303	$ 9
Episcopalian	44	60	74
Lutheran	99	40	27
Methodist	57	78	58

Source: Appendix A.9

programs—$290 and $303 respectively. By contrast, the Protestant judicatories averaged $67 and $59 for the two program areas.

Insurance, Retirement, and Other

The insurance expenditures at the diocese, synod, or conference level (both personal and medical insurance) are quite high. See Table 3.10. The Methodist conferences spent an average of $1,162 per active clergy, the Episcopal dioceses averaged $457, and the Catholic dioceses averaged $366. The Lutheran synods, by contrast, spent very little—an average of only $12.

Retirement expenditures at the judicatory level were highest in Methodist conferences, since the Methodists today have a nationwide program of accelerated contributions to denominational pension funds. This accounts for the $2,104 per clergy paid at the conference level. For Catholics the figure is also rather high—$440 per active priest. Otherwise little is contributed at the judicatory level for clergy retirement.

Table 3.10 Support Programs by Diocese, Synod, or Conference Per Active Clergy: Benefits and Other

	Benefits		Other
	Personal & Medical Insurance	Retirement	
Catholic	$ 366	$ 440	$ 19
Episcopalian	457	78	653
Lutheran	12	55	262
Methodist	1,162	2,104	231

Source: Appendix A.9

The "other" expenditures in Table 3.10 include training and support programs for bishops and district superintendents, and mission development costs. Outlays for them are high for Episcopal dioceses—$654 per active clergy—but low for Catholic dioceses, Lutheran synods, and Methodist conferences.[5]

Total Support Per Clergy

Table 3.11 summarizes the cost of full-time clergy at the local and judicatory levels. The second column also includes support costs at the *national* as well as the judicatory level. We investigated programs funded at the national level and found some only for Lutherans and Methodists, where modest sums are expended for clergy continuing education—an average of $12 per clergy for the United Methodist Church and an average of $21 for the Lutheran Church in America. (See appendix Table A.7.)

The fourth column is the expenditure at the judicatory and national level for seminary education of the next generation of clergy. In all the denominations, judicatories expend large amounts of money to support seminary training for future clergy. In the United Methodist Church there is also a national (in addition to judicatory) subsidy amounting to $286 per active clergy in

1986. In the Lutheran Church in America the same is the case, amounting to $36 per active clergy.

These expenditures for seminary training are low, partly because the total expenses of seminary are borne by numerous parties, including the students themselves, parishes helping them, and seminary endowments.[6]

The first column of Table 3.11 is the total cost of clergy at the parish level (from Table 3.4), and the second is the total cost at the judicatory and national levels. The third is the total cost if the seminary education of future clergy is not included. (Analysts debate if the cost of educating future clergy should be included at this point.) If the education of future clergy *is* to be included, read the fifth column, which is probably the most credible estimate of the average total institutional cost of hiring full-time clergy. The Episcopalian figure is highest at $42,750. Next highest are the Lutheran figure ($40,061) and the Methodist figure ($39,581), and the Catholic figure is by far the lowest ($28,651).

Table 3.11 Compensation and Support Cost Per Active Clergy, with Seminary Education Cost and Grand Total

	Total Parish + Compensation	Support = Costs	Total Cost Per Clergy	+	Seminary = Education	Grand Total
Catholic	$26,184	$1,428	$27,612		$1,039	$28,651
Episcopalian	41,029	1,366	42,395		355	42,750
Lutheran	39,059	493	39,552		509	40,061
Methodist	35,308	3,690	38,998		583	39,581

Source: Appendix A.5 and A.9

Costs of Part-Time Ordained Clergy

Our study also gathered data on 62 part-time clergy who were serving in the sample parishes. A "part-time" clergy was defined as someone who held another position in a diocese, synod, or conference office, who was semi-retired, or who was functioning as a pastor part-time while holding a secular position. Clergy working full-time in yoked parishes were not included. In our data part-timers comprised 19 percent of the ordained clergy.

Information on part-time clergy is only moderately useful, since these persons' job descriptions vary. Their compensation is of course related to the hours they work per week. In our sample the Catholic part-time priests averaged 10 hours a week in the parish, and the Episcopalian part-time priests averaged 19 hours. The Lutherans averaged 22 hours a week, and the Methodists 25 hours. Their total compensation is summarized in Table 3.12. The total amounts vary little from denomination to denomination, even though the Lutherans and Methodists serve more hours a week.

Table 3.12 Average Total Compensation for Part-Time Clergy

	Average Hours Per Week	Total Compensation	=	Dollar Income	+	Housing & All Benefits
Catholic	10	$11,410		$6,833		$4,577
Episcopalian	19	10,132		6,099		4,033
Lutheran	22	11,118		5,213		5,905
Methodist	25	12,185		7,634		4,551

Housing is provided by the parish for 42 percent of these part-time Catholic priests, 31 percent of the Episcopalians, 62 percent of the Lutherans, and 53 percent of the Methodists. The figures in Table 3.12 include all housing costs regardless of whether the clergy owned their homes or not.

These part-time clergy are essential for keeping many small parishes open. Sixty percent of them are staffing small parishes unable to have a full-time pastor.

4.

Cost of Non-Ordained Professional Ministers

We turn to the finances of hiring non-ordained professionals to carry out ministry in parishes. In the Catholic community they are of two distinct types which have very different financial arrangements—vowed religious sisters and lay persons. We will discuss them separately, beginning with the sisters. Then we will look at lay persons, both Catholic and Protestant.

Full-Time Catholic Religious Sisters

Religious sisters occupy a position between the ordained priest and the professional lay minister. They take vows, live celibate lives, and dedicate themselves life-long to serve the church. In some areas of the United States they have been given responsibility for administering parishes. Traditionally sisters have received very low incomes. Today, because of the rising numbers of retired sisters requiring financial support by their communities, income for working sisters has become a serious issue in the Roman Catholic Church (see *Wall Street Journal*, 1986). Sisters' salaries have risen but still they are low.

61

In our 1987 study we found only 25 full-time sisters working in the 62 Catholic parishes studied. They were employed mainly as educators or as pastoral associates. Data on 25 cases is barely adequate for making general conclusions, and we caution the reader about drawing too-precise implications from our data.

Total Compensation

Table 4.1 shows the total compensation of the full-time sisters. The average was $15,120, including an average dollar income of $10,103. Their income was about 20 percent higher in the Western states than in the Northeast or Southeast.

Table 4.1 Average Total Compensation for Catholic Religious Women Full-Time in Parish Ministry

	Number	Total = Compensation	Dollar Income	+ Housing & All Benefits
National Average	25	$15,120	$10,103	$5,017
By Region of Country:				
Northeast	7	14,215	7,938	6,277
Southeast	9	14,212	9,289	4,923
West	9	17,136	13,891	3,245

Source: Appendix A.10

The last column in Table 4.1 gives the value of housing and all other benefits provided. A housing allowance was provided for almost every religious sister in the Southeast (93 percent) but for only 13 percent in the West; in the Northeast it was provided for 73 percent. Actual housing was provided by parishes to about one-half of the sisters in the Northeast and one-third in the Southeast, but none in the West. Housing cost figures in the table are averages across all of the sisters, whether or not they received housing allowances or actual housing; in the latter case we used the fair rental value of the space.

Allowances and Benefits

We found a wide variation in allowances and benefits, as Table 4.2 indicates. The average travel allowance was $1,906.

Table 4.2 Average Allowances & Benefits for Catholic Religious Women Full-Time in Parish Ministry*

	Number	Allowances		Benefits	
		Travel	Education	Retirement	Health
National Average	25	$1,906	$419	$784	$1,103
By Region of Country:					
Northeast	7	3,141	292	408	960
Southeast	9	1,275	547	250	975
West	9	1,084	326	1,047	1,059

* For those receiving allowances and/or benefits
Source: Appendix A.10

The highest travel allowances were in the Northeast, averaging over $3,100; they were lowest in the West. About two-thirds of the parishes we studied (64 percent) provided a travel allowance to full-time sisters. The average education allowance was $419; 56 percent of the sisters received one.

Retirement benefits averaged $784, and a little less than two-thirds received them. They were much higher in the West ($1,047) than in the Northeast ($408) or Southeast ($250). About one-sixth of the Western parishes (17 percent) paid the sisters' share of social security payments. Health benefits averaged $1,103, with little difference between the three regions of the nation; 64 percent received them.

Are these sisters more commonly found in single-clergy parishes or multi-clergy parishes? Of the 25, twenty were working in multi-clergy parishes, three were working in single-clergy parishes and two were administering priestless parishes. No one should think that the sisters are "filling in" where priests are absent or too few in number; given the realities of parish finances, they are most often hired in large parishes with multiple priests on staff. As we shall see below, their financial burden in these large parishes was minimal—they cost a parish an average of only $8 per household per year.

Full-Time Lay Professional Ministers

The concept "lay minister" is currently in flux, and during our data gathering we were faced with questions of exactly whom it encompasses. We included the most standard ministries, stressing that the persons had to be carrying out personal religious ministry to individuals or groups in the parish. We left the final decision of whom to include or exclude to the local pastor, who best knew the persons and their work. The types of ministry we identified were:

Director of Christian Education

Worship Director

Organist

Music Director

Pastoral Associate

Youth Director

Administrative Assistant

Other

Table 4.3 Total Number of Lay Professionals by Denomination

	Number of Parishes	Number of Lay Professionals	
		Full-Time	Part-Time
Catholic	62	66	63
Episcopalian	46	31	32
Lutheran	46	17	53
Methodist	47	22	55
Total	201	136	203

Source: Appendix A.12 for full-time lay staff

We left the definition of "administrative assistant" broad enough to cover a business administrator, executive assistant or similar job, so long as the person is directly ministering to people in the parish.

In which denominations are these persons serving? Table 4.3 provides a summary. Of the 136 full-time lay professionals (not including Catholic sisters) we found, the largest number were employed by the Catholic Church. While Catholic parishes comprised only 31 percent of those in our study, they hired 49 percent of the full-time lay professionals and 31 percent of the part-time. (If we include full-time Catholic religious women, the Catholic parishes employed 57 percent of the total.) The full-time lay professional is disproportionately a Catholic phenomenon, most commonly in larger parishes. About three-fourths of all the full-time lay professionals worked in parishes with two or more full-time clergy, suggesting that lay ministers typically serve *in addition to* ordained clergy, not in place of them.

Total Compensation for Full-Time Lay Professionals

Table 4.4 and Figure 4.1 depict national average compensation for full-time lay professionals. (We made no attempt to gather data by sex, but the majority of lay professionals today are women.)

The average total compensation was $19,818 for Catholics, $16,754 for Episcopalians, $19,463 for Lutherans, and $23,247 for Methodists. There was much variation, with 35 percent of the lay professionals in all denominations receiving $20,000 to $24,999, and another 18 percent receiving more than $25,000. At the lower end, 31 percent received between $15,000 and $19,999, and 22 percent received under $15,000.

Very few of the lay professionals received a housing allowance—only 11 percent of the Catholics, 13 percent of the Episcopalians, 6 percent of the Lutherans, and 18 percent of the Methodists. Less than 4 percent lived in parish-provided housing. A wide variation exists regarding payment of social security and workmen's compensation insurance. Ninety-one percent of the Catholics had this paid by the parish, compared with 65 per-

Table 4.4 Average Total Compensation for Full-Time Lay Professionals Showing Compensation, Dollar Income, Allowance and Benefits*

	Full-Time Lay Staff	Total = Compensation	Dollar + Income	Allowances & Benefits
Catholic	66	$19,818	$16,061	$3,757
Episcopalian	31	16,754	13,532	3,222
Lutheran	17	19,463	15,978	3,485
Methodist	22	23,247	18,632	4,615

* For those receiving allowances and/or benefits
Source: Appendix A.12

Figure 4.1
Average Lay Minister Total Compensation

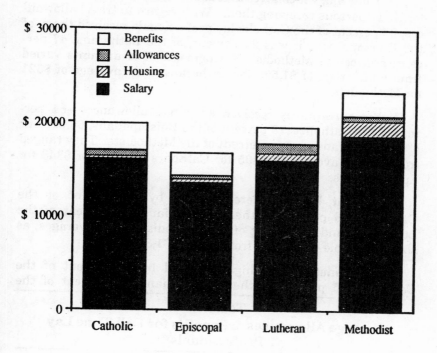

Note: Not all receive allowances and benefits.

cent for the Episcopalians, 47 percent for the Lutherans, and 59 percent for the Methodists.

Compensation of lay professionals varies by region. It was highest in the Southeast, where the average was $19,465. In the West the average was $17,780, and in the Northeast the figure was about $15,000 or $16,000 (an estimate due to the paucity of cases).

Allowances and Benefits for Full-Time Lay Professionals

See Table 4.5, which gives amounts of allowances and benefits for those persons receiving them. With regard to travel allowances, 35 percent of the Catholic lay professionals received them; of the Episcopalians, it was 23 percent; of the Lutherans, 47 percent; and of the Methodists, 32 percent. The amounts varied from an average of $1,563 for Lutherans to an average of $521 for Methodists.

Higher percentages received education allowances—64 percent of the Catholics, 23 percent of the Episcopalians, 65 percent of the Lutherans, and 55 percent of the Methodists. They ranged from a high average of $495 for Catholics to a low of $348 for Episcopalians.

Retirement benefits were received by 68 percent of the Catholics, 26 percent of the Episcopalians, 18 percent of the Lutherans, and 45 percent of the Methodists. The averages, as shown in Table 4.5, varied from $958 to $1,805.

Health benefits were high, received by 85 percent of the Catholics, 65 percent of the Episcopalians, 47 percent of the

Table 4.5
Average Allowances & Benefits for Full-Time Lay Professionals*

| | Allowances | | Benefits | |
	Travel	Education	Retirement	Health
Catholic	$710	$495	$958	$1,255
Episcopalian	1,256	348	1,457	1,984
Lutheran	1,563	487	1,805	1,005
Methodist	521	461	1,621	1,089

* For those receiving allowances and/or benefits
Source: Appendix A.12

Lutherans, and 86 percent of the Methodists, with amounts ranging from $1,005 for the Lutherans to $1,984 for the Episcopalians.

Social security or workmen's compensation were paid by the parish for 91 percent of the Catholics, 65 percent of the Episcopalians, 47 percent of the Lutherans, and 59 percent of the Methodists, with amounts ranging from $991 for the Episcopalians to $1,438 for the Methodists. (See appendix Table A.12.)

We found wide regional differences regarding retirement benefits. Western parishes paid the most, averaging $1,436, whereas the Southeastern and Northeastern parishes averaged only $575 and $257 respectively. In the West the Methodist parishes extended the highest benefits, averaging $2,172. Variations in health benefits were small from region to region.

Compensation of Lay Professionals Per Household

How much does a lay professional cost a parish per household, when all salary and benefit figures are added up? The data are in Table 4.6. Again we see that the cost is lower for Catholics than for Protestants, just as it was for ordained clergy. The

Table 4.6 Average Cost Per Household for Compensation of Full-Time Lay Professionals

	National Average	By Number of Clergy		
		Two or More	One	None
Catholic	$15	$14	$21	--
Episcopalian	44	43	48	--
Lutheran	61	56	74	--
Methodist	24	22	65	--

Source: Appendix A.13

member-to-staff ratio in the Catholic Church is much higher than in the Protestant denominations. In Table 4.6 we see that the average Catholic household pays only $15 for an average lay professional. In the Episcopal Church the figure is $44, in the Lutheran Church, $61, and in the Methodist Church, $24. And as we noted earlier, smaller parishes pay more per person for their leadership; the third column shows somewhat higher per-household figures in single-clergy parishes.

Types of Ministry

What types of ministry are the parishes employing lay professionals to perform? Table 4.7 shows the distribution within each denomination (excluding Catholic religious sisters). Already we have mentioned the large number of full-time lay ministers in the Catholic parishes. The largest number are working as directors of Christian Education, and many are also working as pastoral associates, administrative assistants or youth directors. In the Episcopal Church a large number are working as administrative assistants.

Table 4.7 Distribution of Full-Time Lay Professional Ministers by Denomination & Type of Ministry

| | Catholic | | | Epis-copal | Luth-eran | Metho-dist |
	Lay	Religious	Total			
Christian Education	21	9	30	1	4	4
Youth Director	10	2	12	1	2	5
Worship Director	3	1	4	--	--	1
Music Director	7	1	8	3	--	6
Organist	1	1	2	4	--	1
Admin. Asst.	13	--	13	14	4	3
Pastoral Assoc.	4	9	13	1	4	--
Other	7	1	9	7	3	2
Total	66	25	90	31	17	22

Source: Appendix A.17

Total Compensation by Type of Ministry

The average total compensation for persons performing the different types of ministry is shown in Table 4.8. The table does not include Catholic religious women, and it does not break down the data by denomination because of small numbers of cases.

Only four categories of lay ministers received an average total compensation over $20,000—Christian education directors, youth directors, music directors, and pastoral associates.

The last three columns of Table 4.8 include only those persons receiving the benefits. In the case of social security (FICA) and workmen's compensation, only about three-fourths of the lay professionals have their payments made by the parish. (The figures shown are the average amount for them.) Retirement benefits are received by 50 percent of Christian educators, 61 percent of youth directors, 63 percent of music directors, and 41 percent of administrative assistants. (Figures for smaller categories are in appendix Table A.17.) Health benefits are

Table 4.8 Average Total Compensation for Full-Time Lay Professional Ministers by Type of Ministry, Showing Dollar Income & Benefits*

	Total Compensation	Dollar Income	FICA & Other	Benefits Retirement	Health
Christian Education	$20,048	$16,146	$1,163	$1,144	$1,294
Youth Director	20,925	16,594	1,313	838	1,195
Worship Director	19,888	16,631	1,181	1,059	1,006
Music Director	23,402	19,219	1,129	1,291	1,581
Organist	13,860	11,583	1,106	1,500	1,842
Admin. Asst.	19,668	16,745	1,168	1,275	1,434
Pastoral Assoc.	20,164	14,810	1,418	995	1,376
Other	16,862	12,881	1,068	1,301	1,005

*For those receiving benefits. Source: Appendix A.16.1

received by 70 percent of the Christian educators, 94 percent of the youth directors, 88 percent of the music directors, and 71 percent of the administrative assistants.[1]

Part-Time Lay Professional Ministers

The definition of "lay minister" in our study was the same for full-time and part-time ministers. To be included, a person had to have received at least $2,000 from the parish in the last year. Part-time lay ministers fulfilled the types of ministry shown in Table 4.9. A large number were either music directors or organists—61 percent.

Their compensation varied greatly, depending on hours worked per week or type of service. Table 4.10 summarizes what we found with regard to total compensation, dollar income, hours worked per week, and wages per hours. Lay ministers serving in the areas of Sunday worship or liturgy received total compensa-

Table 4.9 Distribution of Part-Time Lay Professional Ministers by Denomination & Type of Ministry

	Catholic	Episcopal	Lutheran	Methodist
Christian Education	12	4	1	5
Youth Director	8	1	2	4
Worship Director	3	--	1	1
Music Director	12	14	19	19
Organist	21	11	19	17
Admin. Asst.	4	--	2	--
Pastoral Assoc.	10	--	3	2
Other	7	2	6	7
Total	77	32	53	55

Table 4.10 Average Total Compensation for Part-Time Professional Ministers By Type of Ministry, Showing Average Hours Worked & Wage Per Hour

	Total Compensation	Dollar Income	Average Per Week	Hours Wage
Christian Education	$8,952	$8,046	21	$8.02
Youth Director	6,552	5,843	18	6.86
Worship Director	6,409	5,556	15	8.44
Music Director	5,732	5,298	10	10.60
Organist	5,654	5,246	10	11.45
Admin. Asst.	10,302	9,268	24	8.37
Pastoral Assoc.	8,822	6,119	17	9.98
Other	6,192	4,358	13	10.65

tion averaging a little over $10 per hour. Lowest paid were youth directors and administrative assistants.

Trained part-time lay ministers will play an important role in the future, since their services are modest in cost and they are becoming more and more available.

Part Three

Effectiveness of Professional Parish Leadership

5.

Lay Leaders' Attitudes About Professional Parish Leadership

American denominations are faced with leadership issues demanding experimentation and new solutions. One primary consideration when scanning the options is *cost*, for no options are possible if they are too expensive. The last two chapters have looked at the cost of several types of leadership. A second consideration is *effectiveness.* Are part-time ordained clergy generally more effective than full-time lay ministers? Are clergy serving one parish full-time generally more effective than those serving two or more parishes and dividing their time between them?

The 1987 research project needed some measures of effectiveness, so we decided to survey the elected lay leaders in each parish, getting their views about the effectiveness of their professional leadership and their attitudes on leadership issues in general. The elected lay leaders, we felt, would be the most crucial persons among the laity of each parish.

How should a researcher measure effectiveness? It is a matter of subjective judgment, and it inevitably varies among persons in the parish and among lay persons, clergy and denominational leaders. By limiting our research to the elected lay leaders in the parishes we are of course limiting ourselves to *their* assessments of effectiveness. We realize it is not the whole picture, and we make no claim that the attitudes of elected lay leaders are a measure of true effectiveness.

As we enrolled each of the parishes in the research study, we asked for the names of the members of the highest lay committee. In the Catholic parishes this was the parish council; in the Episcopal parishes, the vestry; in the Lutheran parishes, the church council; and in the Methodist parishes, the administrative board. Sociologically these boards vary little from denomination to denomination, though they vary in the amount of constitutional power they have. We sent out 640 questionnaires to Catholic lay leaders, 516 to Episcopal, 525 to Lutheran, and 528 to Methodist.

When we pretested the questionnaires ahead of time, we learned that terminology varied from denomination to denomination so greatly that some of the words and phrases needed to encompass all four were unbearably awkward. To make matters easier for everyone, we changed the Catholic version of the questionnaire into simpler, more direct Catholic terminology. For example, instead of "congregation or parish" we simply used "parish." Instead of "ordained pastor" we simply used "priest."

To encourage returns we cut down the final version of the questionnaire to seven pages, and we did not ask anyone to sign his or her name. In addition to the normal payment to each parish for participation, we offered a bonus of $30 to any parish which successfully returned all of its lay questionnaires. We talked about the bonus in a humorous vein while also conveying that we were serious about getting a good response rate. The incentives worked. We received 543 useable Catholic questionnaires (85 percent), 415 Episcopal questionnaires (80 percent), 442 Lutheran questionnaires (84 percent), and 429 Methodist questionnaires (81 percent). The overall return rate was 83 percent.

We will review the findings under three headings. First, who are these elected lay leaders? Second, how do they rate their parishes and the parish leadership? Third, what are their general views about ordained and lay professional leadership?

Who Are the Elected Lay Leaders?

We asked the lay leaders several questions about themselves. First, how many are men and how many are women? In the Protestant churches over half were men (Episcopals, 62 percent men; Lutherans, 59 percent; Methodists, 51 percent), but among the Catholics only 46 percent were men.

Second, what is their education level? The majority were college graduates—49 percent of the Catholics, 60 percent of the Episcopals, 60 percent of the Lutherans, and 54 percent of the

Methodists. The percentage with post-college education (graduate or professional) was 26 for the Catholics, 32 for the Episcopals, 27 for the Lutherans, and 28 for the Methodists. In all four denominations the men were more educated than the women. Among the Catholics 60 percent of the men leaders and 40 percent of the women leaders were college graduates; among the Episcopals it was 66 percent of the men, 50 percent of the women; among the Lutherans, 69 percent and 48 percent; among the Methodists, 67 percent and 41 percent.

Third, how many have been members of other denominations in the past? We found many of the Protestants had been. Among the Episcopals, 54 percent had; among the Lutherans, 44 percent; among the Methodists, 47 percent. But among the Catholics it was only 13 percent. In all cases the former denominations varied widely, with little pattern except for the large numbers of ex-Baptists.

We looked at variation from geographic region to geographic region, and we found that only in the Catholic community was there some educational difference. Catholics in the West (Colorado and Washington state) had higher levels of education; 60 percent were college graduates, compared with 43 percent in the South and 49 percent in the East.

Ratings of Parishes and Parish Leadership

Parish Morale and Involvement

The questionnaire asked the lay leaders about the morale of the parish members and the financial health of their parishes. See Table 5.1, top part. The table shows the attitudes of lay leaders within each of the three patterns of parish leadership—

Table 5.1
Ratings of Parish Morale and Participation (Percents)

	Catholic			Episcopal			Lutheran			Methodist		
	2+ F-Time	1 F-Time	0 F-Time	2+ F-Time	1 F-Time	0 F-Time	2+ F-Time	1 F-Time	0 F-Time	2+ F-Time	1 F-Time	0 F-Time
Parish morale is "high"	24	27	17	29	36	32	28	36	37	44	26	21
Parish financial health is "excellent" or "good"	55	37	41	62	50	28	49	50	23	52	29	45
Description of the amount of lay involvement in the parish:												
A few active lay people, but most are Sunday-morning only.	5	11	25	3	9	34	2	9	11	5	7	17
Several active boards, but only a small percentage of members are involved.	60	68	47	51	53	27	51	55	39	42	60	50
An active majority of the members are involved in boards, committees, and programs.	35	22	29	46	38	39	47	36	50	54	33	34
Important decisions about the parish life are rarely made without open discussion by church leaders and members. Agree, or Moderately Agree.	67	73	86	73	79	92	90	89	95	85	89	86

multiple ordained clergy, single ordained clergy, and no full-time clergy.

The first question was on the "current morale of the members," and the possible responses were "high," "moderately high," "moderately low," and "low." Most respondents chose "high" or "moderately high," so that the total of the two was about 90 percent in all four denominations. But the percentage saying "high" varied quite a bit, as Table 5.1 shows. It was similar in the three Protestant denominations but a bit lower for Catholics. Among the Methodists the percent reporting high morale was affected by the type of parish leadership—it was higher in parishes having multiple clergy than in the others, and it was lowest in parishes without full-time clergy.[1] (If we total "high" and "moderately high," the Methodist responses do not differ by type of leadership.) For Catholics, Episcopalians and Lutherans, the level of morale is similar in the different size parishes.

The reports of financial health are in the second line of Table 5.1. Among the four denominations there are no overall differences, but in all four the parishes with multiple clergy have the best financial health. These parishes tend to be in more stable and affluent communities. In all the other parishes, not over 50 percent of the lay leaders see their financial health as excellent or good. Also for some reason the Episcopal and Lutheran parishes without full-time clergy are in much worse financial health than the other Episcopal and Lutheran parishes.

The rest of Table 5.1 shows responses to two questions about lay participation in parish leadership. The first had three responses, which are shown in the middle of the table. In all the denominations, the more clergy in the parish, the more the lay persons are involved in parish leadership. (The pattern is weak for the Lutherans.) In all four, multiple-clergy parishes have the highest level of lay involvement, and parishes without full-time clergy have the lowest. This is partly because small Protestant parishes are often "preaching stations" only, without much program in which the members could get involved.

Of the four denominations, the Catholics have the lowest overall level of lay involvement in parish leadership. The combined percent saying that "an active majority of the members are involved..." was 41 for the Episcopal, 42 for the Lutherans, 40 for the Methodists, but only 29 for the Catholics.

The last item in the table is about whether important parish decisions are made without open discussion involving members. Overall, the amount of open discussion reported was lowest among the Catholics; the combined percentage agreeing or moderately agreeing with the statement was 73 for the Catholics, 80 for the Episcopalians, 90 for the Lutherans, and 87 for the Methodists. (These summary figures are not in the table.)

Furthermore, for Catholics and Episcopalians, the more clergy in any parish, the less (on average) open discussion of parish decisions. Apparently the least open discussion of parish decisions takes place in multi-staff Catholic and Episcopalian parishes, and the most takes place in Lutheran and Methodist parishes of all sizes.

Ratings of Specific Leadership Tasks

The questionnaire listed twelve specific leadership tasks and asked the lay leaders to make two ratings—(a) the importance of the tasks ("very," "moderate," or "not very"), and (b) the effectiveness of the current parish staff, both ordained and lay, in carrying them out ("quite," "somewhat," or "not very effective"). If no staff person was doing the task, the respondent circled another response saying so, and the case was eliminated from the calculations of effectiveness.

The results are in Figure 5.1. It portrays the percentage saying that the task was "very important" and the staff was "quite effective." The difference between the two is a rough indication of the gap between desire and reality felt by these lay leaders. (The actual data are shown in the Appendix, Table A.21.)

In Figure 5.1 the dots show the percentage in all four denominations who see each task as "very important," and the vertical bars show the percentage in all four saying the staffs are "very effective." The tasks are arranged in order of importance. Note that the most important tasks are "preaching," "deepening parishioners' spiritual lives," "planning or leading the Sunday

Figure 5.1

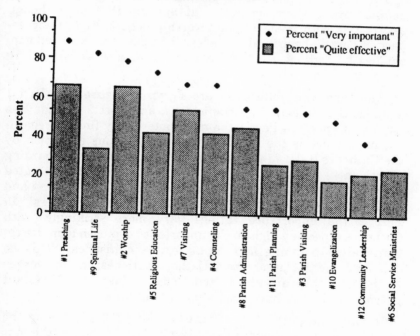

liturgy or worship," and "directing religious education," in that order. Six of the twelve tasks are rated much higher than the others; the important six are all in the realm of preaching, worship, religious education and pastoral care. The less important six have to do with parish planning, administration, evangelization, and social ministries.

The difference between importance and effectiveness on any of the tasks is a rough measure of satisfaction felt by the lay leaders. A gap near the left end of the figure is probably more important, since it occurs on a task seen as crucial. A notable gap is on task #9, "deepening parishioners' spiritual life." The lay leaders are not very happy with staff performance in aiding spiritual life, and this is an important finding in our survey with definite practical implications. It appears that even though satisfaction with preaching and worship is quite high, their impact on personal spiritual life is less than desired. A second gap, smaller but still worthy of mention, is on task #5, "directing religious education."

Denominational differences are shown in Figure 5.2. Part 1 includes the six most important tasks, and Part 2 has the less important ones. In Part 1 the most noteworthy finding regarding importance is the high rating given religious education by the Catholics (task #5). The most noteworthy finding regarding effectiveness is that on five of the six tasks, the Catholics rated their staffs lowest of our four denominations. The Lutheran and Methodist staffs are rated slightly better than the others. In Part 2 the importance ratings vary more strikingly, with Catholics especially high on the importance of parish administration, parish planning and social service ministries. This no doubt reflects the larger size of Catholic parishes; on the average in the U.S. they are almost ten times as large as Protestant parishes and hence have more administrative needs.

In sum: the patterns in Figures 5.1 and 5.2 are among the most important findings in our survey. Lay leaders in the four

Figure 5.2, Part 1

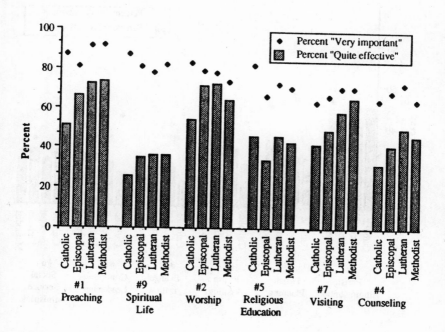

Figure 5.2, Part 2

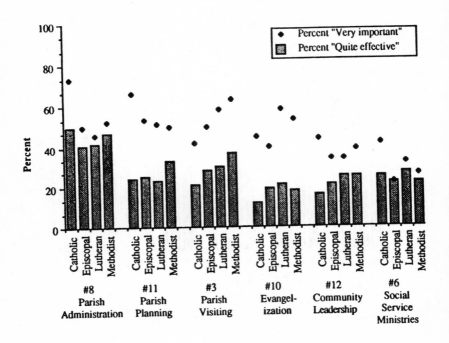

denominations agreed fairly well on the importance of the various leadership tasks, and they agreed quite well when rating the importance of the six most important. (The biggest disagreements were on the less important six.) They agreed moderately well on how well their parish staffs were carrying them out—with Lutheran and Methodist staffs getting better than average ratings and Catholic staffs getting poorer than average. Most striking was the low effectiveness rating on "deepening parishioners' spiritual lives." Why this was so low deserves more investigation than we can do here.

Are there differences in ratings in parishes having different patterns of clerical staffing? For example, are staffs which include no full-time clergy rated lower? Table 5.2 gives the patterns; for easier reading it shows only differences of 12 percentage points or more in effectiveness ratings. The patterns are more mixed than we anticipated, with no clear signal in the Catholic, Episcopal, and Lutheran responses. In general, Catholics rate parish leadership slightly lower when there is no full-time priest, but Episcopalians and Lutherans do not. But among the Methodists there is a clear pattern: they rate the multiple-clergy staffs best and the staffs including less than a full-time clergy as worst. The reason for this Methodist pattern cannot be discerned from our data; it is not because the Methodist lay leaders were different in education than the other lay leaders. Possibly it is because the United Methodist Church has greater variation in levels of clergy training than the other denominations studied here; it has a relatively large number of ministers without seminary degrees, and they tend to serve small congregations. This may be the explanation.

Table 5.2 helps answer the question of whether part-time clergy can minister as effectively as full-time. If they can, we would not expect differences between the second and third column under each denomination. The answer is that there is no noteworthy difference for the Catholics, Episcopalians, and

Table 5.2
Effectiveness of Staff Within Each Pattern of Parish Leadership (Percents)

Current parish staff (ordained or lay) is "quite effective."

	Catholic			Episcopal			Lutheran			Methodist		
	2+ F-Time	1 F-Time	0 F-Time	2+ F-Time	1 F-Time	0 F-Time	2+ F-Time	1 F-Time	0 F-Time	2+ F-Time	1 F-Time	0 F-Time
1. Preaching	43	58	54	-*	·	·	·	·	·	·	·	·
2. Planning or leading the Sunday liturgy or worship	·	·	·	·	·	·	·	·	·	·	·	·
3. Parish visiting	·	·	·	21	30	35	·	·	·	50	31	32
4. Pastoral counseling	32	36	37	·	·	·	·	·	·	52	46	38
5. Directing religious education	·	·	·	·	·	·	·	·	·	54	40	33
6. Directing social service ministries	28	25	16	·	·	·	·	·	·	24	26	14
7. Hospital/shut-in visiting	50	37	35	·	·	·	53	64	51	73	58	64
8. Parish administration	·	·	·	·	·	·	·	·	·	60	45	34
9. Deepening parishioners' spiritual lives	·	·	·	·	·	·	·	·	·	·	·	·
10. Parish evangelization	·	·	·	·	·	·	14	20	33	24	17	11
11. Long-range parish planning	·	·	·	·	·	·	·	·	·	48	29	20
12. Leadership in the neighborhood or community	·	·	·	·	·	·	23	23	36	·	·	·

*Differences of less than 12 percentage points are not shown.

Lutherans; part-time staffs seem to do well. But for the Methodists the part-time staffs are not doing as well.

Locus of Parish Influence

One source of satisfaction or dissatisfaction among church laity is whether they feel that power and influence in the parish are properly distributed and handled. To see if feelings about the proper or improper wielding of influence relate to feelings about satisfaction with leadership, we included a series of questions in the questionnaire, asking the lay leaders to report on who *has* the most "say" or influence in deciding parish policies and programs, and who *ought to have* the most. See Table 5.3. The table gives percentages of who is perceived to have the most influence and who ought to have it, plus a difference between *is* and *ought* (with a positive number indicating more than there ought to be and a negative number indicating less than there ought to be).

In all denominations, the pastors have the most influence in parish life. Over ninety percent of the lay leaders report that the pastors have great or very great influence. In Catholic parishes, the diocese comes a distant second, followed by other staff and the parish council. In Protestant parishes, the lay governing board comes a close second and the staff comes in a distant third.

Attitudes of lay leaders about who *ought to* have the most influence do not always match their views about who *has* it. There is general agreement that the pastors should have the most influence. But there is a mismatch in that "a majority of the church membership" is seen to have much less influence than it should have, and this is the feeling in all four denominations. An overall 57 percent of the lay leaders said that a majority of the membership should have great influence (see item #4 in Table 5.3). Also a smaller mismatch is found in all four denominations, that "one or more powerful individuals in the congregation/parish" have too much influence. Besides these two, the

Table 5.3
Who Has Influence in the Parish? (Percents)

How much "say" or influence do you think that each of the following persons or groups has in determining the policies and programs of this congregation/parish? "Very great" or "Great."

How much "say" or influence do you think each ought to have? "Very great" or "Great."

		Catholic	Episcopal	Lutheran	Methodist
1. The pastor	Has	95	96	95	92
	Ought to have	89	92	92	88
	Difference	--*	--	--	--
2. Other staff (skip if none)					
	Has	55	42	49	48
	Ought to have	54	37	51	51
	Difference	--	--	--	--
3. Governing board/parish council					
	Has	53	85	89	83
	Ought to have	74	90	93	88
	Difference	-21	--	--	--
4. A majority of the church membership (excluding the governing board)					
	Has	17	28	46	27
	Ought to have	41	56	74	59
	Difference	-24	-28	-28	-32
5. One or more powerful individuals in the congregation/parish					
	Has	19	17	18	25
	Ought to have	4	5	5	5
	Difference	15	12	13	20
6. The diocese/synod/conference					
	Has	66	37	23	32
	Ought to have	44	33	17	25
	Difference	22	--	--	--
7. Yourself	Has	13	19	23	16
	Ought to have	16	16	21	12
	Difference	--	--	--	--

*Differences of less than 12 percentage points are not shown.

only perceived problems are in the Catholic Church, where the lay leaders think the parish councils have too little influence and the diocese has too much. The differences on these two items among the Catholic lay leaders are fairly large, revealing some widespread feelings. Many of the Catholic lay leaders would like to see some of the power of the diocese transferred to the local parish council.

The overall pattern is a kind of convergence, in that the major differences between Catholics and Protestants are exactly on the power structures seen by the Catholics as most needing change—in short, the dioceses at present have too much influence and the local parish councils have too little. The feelings about legitimate authority are more similar across the four denominations than are the current institutional practices.

We wondered if the views in Table 5.3 would vary according to whether a parish had multiple clergy, a single clergy, or less than a full-time clergy. We looked at the data and found no clear differences, hence the figures are not shown here.

Ordained or Lay Leadership

Table 5.4 reports levels of agreement with five statements about one's own parish. The first says that the average lay person "responds better to the leadership of someone who is ordained" (Catholic version: "to a priest"). The majority in all four denominations said it was true. The second statement is on the same topic; it says that if a full-time ordained clergy (or priest) could not be secured, parish morale would drop. Again the majority in all four denominations said it was true. These findings send a clear signal—that in all four denominations lay people have a high regard for ordained clergy and want them in their parishes.

Many respondents wrote in comments in their desire for full-time clergy. A Catholic in New Hampshire wrote:

Table 5.4
Descriptions of One's Own Parish (Percents)

Is each of the following true of your congregation or parish? "Usually true."*

	Catholic	Episcopal	Lutheran	Methodist
1. The average lay person in this congregation/parish responds better to the leadership of someone who is *ordained*.**	62	64	52	63
2. If this congregation/parish could not secure a full-time, professionally trained, ordained pastor, the members' morale would be adversely affected.	60	64	58	65
3. Our pastor seems to have more than enough time to accomplish the pastoral tasks required in this congregation or parish.	14	16	11	21
4. The pastor and lay leaders have difficulty in getting members to volunteer their time in helping with the ministry tasks of the congregation or parish.	16	10	20	15
5. There is general satisfaction among the majority of members with our *current* pattern of pastoral leadership.	59	61	74	71

* The questionaire had five responses, "Usually true," "Somewhat true," "Somewhat false," "Usually false," and "Have no opinion."

**The items were changed slightly for the Catholic questionaire; the wording given here is from the Protestant version. For example, item #1 in the Catholic questionaire said "responds bettern to the leadership of a priest."

I feel the role of the lay person will steadily increase, and I'm in favor of this. However, I feel very strongly about having an ordained priest as our spiritual leader, because by his training and ordination he is the "specialist." I can probably balance a budget better than most priests (a housewife, mother of 5) and I'm probably closer to God than some priests. But a priest is a priest, is a priest.

An Episcopalian in Ohio:

Of course lay persons are necessary, but nothing of value can be accomplished without a strong clergy who have been taught to meet the needs of all. If this questionnaire is trying to determine the economic arguments for having lay persons instead of clergy at the head of our parish, I could safely say we would prefer to remunerate our clergy.

A Lutheran in Florida:

In November 1985 Pastor ____ died suddenly and we were without a pastor for one year. We had excellent supply pastors, and the congregation rallied and followed the leadership of the council for one year until we were able to call our present pastor. This is a very stable congregation and could probably function very well under lay leadership, but we would not want to.

A Methodist in Ohio:

It is right and correct that we should minister to each other. However, given a choice I would prefer an ordained minister.

The third and fourth statements in Table 5.5 are about workload. The third states that the pastor has "more than enough time" for his or her tasks. Only an average of 15 percent agreed. The fourth says that the pastor and lay leaders have difficulty in securing enough lay volunteers. Again only about 15 percent agreed. In all the denominations the clergy are seen to have enough work to do, and they have no serious problem finding volunteers.

Many written-in comments attest to the impact of parish clergy on the morale of the people and their willingness to volunteer. For example, a Methodist from Ohio wrote:

We couldn't have chosen any better ministers than those we are fortunate enough to have. Sometimes I wonder where they find the time, the love, and the energy to do all they accomplish. We are a lucky congregation and because of that, our members say yes when they are asked to participate.

A Catholic in New Jersey:

We are a parish of volunteers. Our response has always been strong. However, my feeling is that the response has always been in direct proportion to the popularity of our pastor and staff.

A Methodist in New Hampshire:

As a Methodist for over thirty years, I feel the "tide" of our membership rises and falls with the person in the pulpit. This is also true of the rise and fall of effective membership on various committees.

A Catholic in Ohio:

I believe that our parish priest is doing an excellent job. A lot of these questions depend on the personality of the pastor. If he is a true priest—doesn't drink to excess and do things behind the people's back—then the lay response is better.

A Lutheran in the East tells of the opposite effect:

If a pastoral change is not made real soon in our church, there will be no church! The only satisfied people in our church are the people who do nothing. All the hard workers of the church are very unhappy. The closer you get to our pastor the more you know what little he does. The only things he does well is visit the sick and shut-ins and take a lot of vacations. Also his wife is no help to him or the church.

A Florida Catholic tells of the impact of a change of pastors:

Less than five years ago, I was an ordained deacon, and my wife and I moved into this parish. The parishioners here with our pastor had formed one of the most vibrant, faith-filled, active parishes we could imagine. Now after four years, with a different pastor, we feel almost burned out because we get lots of "yes, let's do it" from the pastor and parishioners but no commitment to really hang in there and keep working "in the name of the Lord" to really accomplish anything that is lasting.

Returning to Table 5.4, the last statement is a kind of summary of satisfaction with the pattern of current leadership. It asks about the "pattern of pastoral leadership," not the incumbent staff members. For many church members this may be a difficult distinction to make when filling out a questionnaire, but we wanted to make it, since our interest is in leadership *structures,* not individual leaders. The responses show that a combined average of about two-thirds in all the denominations feel satisfied. Satisfaction is highest among the Lutherans and lowest among the Catholics and Episcopalians, consistent with other findings reported earlier.

A large number of respondents vented feelings about their ministers and priests in comments written on the questionnaire. Many of the strongest feelings were voiced by Catholics. They ranged from love to anger. A Catholic from Ohio exemplifies the love many felt:

Since Father ____ has come to ____ Parish, we the parish family have been greatly blessed. We were "starving" for that leadership, in his humble manner, and his gifts of sharing his spirituality we so desperately needed. I know he has enriched my spiritual personal life greatly. His daily example and love of God are so enriching. Consequently, more people are offering their volunteer services and really want to serve the needs of their parish. He's pulled us all together and created a family again. I thank God for sending him to us, all the time. We are beginning to grow together spiritually and socially, and it's wonderful. Thank God!

Another Catholic:

Our pastor could use some administrative help but wouldn't accept if offered. He tries to run it all on his own, and I'm sure will get worn out fast. We need new ideas and an American priest that has lived a little in the world. Our pastor is extremely devoted and is very good with spiritual things and extremely compassionate with people suffering, but he tends to stand outside and look in, but not wanting to get attached.

A Methodist told about disillusionment:

I've been a leader in the church for fifteen years from local to general, and to see the action and relationship among the preachers in my conference makes me have mixed feelings about even staying in the church. Someone once said, and this is the way I feel, "It's like Noah's ark; if it wasn't for the storm on the outside you couldn't stand the smell on the inside."

A Catholic from New Jersey:

One of the most disappointing things about our Catholic Church is the lack of dynamic leaders who can help people want to do more for and learn more about the church. We need leaders who will make us want to grow. Our priests must learn how to be better speakers.

We received some passionate comments on ministers and priests who were seen as neglecting their parishes. A Catholic:

Our biggest trouble stems from our pastor concentrating most of his expertise (and he is very good) and energies with matters outside our parish. Travelling, friends from other parishes where he was assigned, ecumenical activities, diocesan duties, all seem to come before the needs of our parish. We need a shepherd all of us, not just a few close friends. We have had many occasions where he is desperately needed and he is too busy.

A Methodist describes a similar problem:

Many people in the congregation feel that our minister's time is spread too wide. We share our pastor with another congregation and the conference. He has been doing his own secretarial work as well as running newsletters and bulletins.

Another Catholic:

In our parish we have a priest who is so involved in other matters and other parishes he has little time for his own people. He is so involved with the chancery and travels, his time is not spent where he should be. We have a very qualified priest, but he doesn't have his priorities in order. He is our parish priest but he is widely known and is always on the go. Two months vacation a year, so-called retreats, a member of the bishop's committee, writing books, etc. Most priests today don't want to do what they were ordained to do. They want deacons and lay people to do all their work so they can do whatever they please. Our priest is not young. He has over 40 years as a priest. I think he feels our church is retirement.

These comments tell us the depth of feelings among laity, but they cannot help us discern overall patterns of lay attitudes. Do they vary according to the number of clergy in the parish? Table 5.5 shows four of the statements from Table 5.4, giving attitudes of the lay leaders according to clergy staffing patterns. Only four

Table 5.5
Breakdowns of Parish Descriptions by Pattern of Parish Leadership (Percents)

Is each of the following true of your congregation or parish? "Usually true."*

	Catholic			Episcopal			Lutheran			Methodist		
	2+ F-Time	1 F-Time	0 F-Time	2+ F-Time	1 F-Time	0 F-Time	2+ F-Time	1 F-Time	0 F-Time	2+ F-Time	1 F-Time	0 F-Time
2. If this congregation/parish could not secure a full-time, professionally trained, ordained pastor, the members' morale would be adversely affected.	64	63	45	66	68	54	66	62	38	68	73	52
3. Our pastor seems to have more than enough time to accomplish the pastoral tasks required in this congregation or parish.	--**	--	--	7	15	32	--	--	--	14	20	28
4. The pastor and lay leaders have difficulty in getting members to volunteer their time in helping with the ministry tasks of the congregation or parish.	--	--	--	--	--	--	--	--	--	7	15	24
5. There is general satisfaction among the majority of the members with our current pattern of pastoral leadership.	--	--	--	50	67	69	--	--	--	77	72	65

*Question #1 is not shown, because no differences occurred in the responses.

**Differences of less than 12 percentage points are not shown.

of the statements are shown, since the first one found no differences.

On statement #2, concerning morale if no full-time clergy could be secured, we see a clear difference between those parishes with a full-time clergy and those without. The lay leaders in parishes without a full-time clergy expect less of a morale drop if no full-time clergy would be available. This is no doubt because *already* they are without a full-time clergy and they are accustomed to it. But the statement has high figures for the two categories of parishes with full-time clergy—higher than we saw earlier. People who now have full-time clergy do not want to lose them, and if they did, they predict that morale would suffer.

Statement #3 has an interesting finding, that the Episcopal and Methodist leaders without full-time clergy disproportionately believe that there is not enough work to keep their parish staff busy.

Statement #4 has differences for only the Methodists, who report that parishes without full-time clergy have a disproportionate amount of trouble getting lay volunteers. Earlier we saw that these Methodist parishes suffer from low morale, and perhaps this is a by-product. These Methodist parishes in our study without full-time clergy averaged 159 members.

Statement #5 has a curious pattern which we cannot explain. In the Episcopal Church the laity without full-time clergy are more satisfied than average, and in the Methodist church the opposite is the case. Among Catholics and Lutherans there are no differences. Why? In any event, there is no *overall* difference in satisfaction with parish leadership because of having or not having full-time clergy, and this is the important message to be gotten. Apparently parish life and parishioners' expectations have a way of adjusting over a period of time to whatever level of clergy leadership there is.

General Views About Ordained and Lay Professional Leadership

If there is a shortage of clergy or of money to employ them, perhaps some of the parish leadership can be carried out by trained lay persons. Whenever this is discussed, many questions are raised. Would laity accept lay professionals carrying out various leadership activities? Would the lay professionals tend to undermine the authority of ordained clergy? Would other laity pull back from volunteering to carry out church tasks? This section reviews several of these topics.

One series of questions listed ministerial activities and asked the respondents if, "given the choice, you would prefer to have an ordained pastor or a trained lay professional performing each of the listed activities." If it would make no difference, there was a place to say that. The results are in Table 5.6. (The nine ministerial activities do not include celebration of the sacraments, which is limited to ordained clergy in all of these denominations.)

The table gives the percentages saying they would prefer an ordained pastor doing each activity. The respondents most want ordained pastors for #2, conducting a funeral, and #1, preaching a sermon. The activities for which ordained pastors are least often preferred are #5, reading the lessons in the worship service, #9, leading adult education classes or Bible study, and #7, managing the organizational affairs of the parish. Probably the most interesting is that Catholics are less concerned than Protestants about whether clergy perform a majority of the tasks. Why is this? Why would the Catholic laity be less concerned if nonordained people carried out central ministerial tasks? Is it because they are less satisfied with their current leadership? Or because they anticipate a shortage of priests in the future? Or because they reject some ontological doctrines about the special

Table 5.6
Preference for an Ordained Pastor (Percents)

For each activity, would you prefer to have an ordained pastor or a trained lay professional perform it? Or indicate if it would make no difference. Percent "Prefer an Ordained Pastor."

	Catholic	Episcopal	Lutheran	Methodist
1. Preaching a sermon	54	76	81	84
2. Conducting a funeral	81	91	93	90
3. Counseling with you about a personal problem or decision	48	58	61	65
4. Leading a pastoral prayer	28	33	45	42
5. Reading the lessons in the worship service	11	6	6	15
6. Visiting you in the hospital	53	57	54	52
7. Managing the organizational affairs of the parish or congregation	21	28	24	36
8. Teaching confirmation or new member classes	24	61	62	64
9. Leading adult education classes or Bible study	20	25	24	24

status of priesthood? We were not at all prepared for this finding, and we cannot explain it.

The table showing breakdowns by pattern of staffing is in the Appendix (Table A.22). The only visible pattern is that among Episcopalians, those without full-time clergy in their parishes disproportionately prefer clergy to carry out many of the activities. The reason for this is unclear.

Lay Professionals

In Table 5.7 there are three statements about lay professionals, to which the respondents were asked to agree or dis-

agree. The first says that most of the tasks currently done by ordained pastors could be done by competent lay persons, and an
average of 58 percent agreed. Agreement was considerably
higher among Catholics than among Protestants (74 percent,
compared with an average of 53 percent); again we see a greater
acceptance of lay professionals by Catholics.

Would the use of paid lay persons in leadership roles undermine the prestige and authority of the pastor? The second statement asked this question, and a little less than half said that it
would. The rest said it would make no difference.

Would the use of paid lay leaders cause other laity to reduce
their willingness to volunteer for church work? On the third
statement an average of 61 percent guessed that this would hap-
pen. The Catholics had the least fear.

Table 5.7
Statements About Lay Professionals

Whether or not your congregation employs a lay professional, please circle
the number between 1 and 4 that best reflects your opinion. Percent "Agree
strongly" or "Agree somewhat."*

	Catholic	Episcopal	Lutheran	Methodist
1. Most of the tasks currently done by ordained pastors can be done equally well by lay persons with special competence for the task.	74	54	56	48
2. Paying trained lay persons to do tasks often done by ordained pastors is likely to undermine the prestige and authority of the pastor.	46	47	44	54
3. Paying trained lay persons to take responsibility for ministry tasks is likely to reduce the willingness of parishioners to volunteer their time to the congregation or parish.	57	63	60	64

*The four responses were "Agree strongly," "Agree somewhat," "Disagree some-
what," and "Disagree strongly."

The table showing variations in opinions according to parish staffing patterns is not shown here, since there were no clear patterns.

Many comments were made on the questionnaires regarding an expansion of professional lay leadership, pro and con. The arguments in favor had definite themes. An Episcopalian from Washington said:

> I believe our priest spends too much time on the day-to-day "housekeeping" tasks. We need an "executive secretary" to do those things, so he can be free to minister. Then we wouldn't need to add an assistant priest. There's plenty of room for both paid and volunteer lay ministry in our parish.

A Catholic from New Hampshire:

> I think trained lay professionals is the way to rejuvenate and activate parish life. I do not see it as a threat to clergy. In fact, freeing clergy to be more effective in use of gifts and talents and true spiritual—not necessarily administrative—leadership.

A Methodist from Washington:

> I feel trained lay people should be used to lead education and youth programs in the church and free up some of the pastor's responsibilities and time. Most pastors in larger churches seem to be spread too thin. And I'm sure the pastors of smaller churches feel this way.

A Catholic from Florida:

> The burden of balancing a budget, or large purchases, or paying the bills should be in the hands of professionals and leave the religious duties to the priests and nuns.

A Methodist from Florida:

While living in Memphis, our Methodist Church there had a paid lay woman that called on the sick, elderly, and shut-ins. On one occasion I was in traction with disc problems when she came bringing strawberries. Through the years I have remembered this small gesture. I believe it is of value if the church can afford it.

Others expressed reservations about lay leadership, mainly that they would encroach on the clergy, that other laity would not accept them adequately, and that the lay leaders would not be capable enough. A Catholic from New Hampshire:

If lay persons are to have a more active role in the ministries of the future Catholic Church, their role will be more widely accepted if they're trained and educated rather than using those "of great faith" in the parish. Educate the leadership to the level of para-professionals, and those of great faith will be the willing volunteers. Education and training will also give a more universal structure and direction.

An Episcopalian from New Jersey:

I am concerned about undermining the role of priest. However, paying a trained lay person for special tasks—such as finances or administration, would be a reasonable idea if the clergyman didn't have a talent for such.

An Episcopalian from Florida:

There comes along occasionally a person of exceptional talent who can work as a professional and assist the minister in his duties. The routine lay leader does not possess the wisdom in dealing with others and needs training. There need to be lay institutes that lay leaders can attend if we want to train them. Even home study courses would help. Some persons can be trained, but very few.

Table 5.8
Options If No Full-Time Clergy Is Available (Percents)

If there were a decline in finances in your congregation/parish, or if a full-time, seminary educated, ordained pastor were not available, which of the following would you most prefer your congregation/parish to employ to provide pastoral leadership? Rank from 1 to 4. Percent first rank:

	Catholic	Episcopal	Lutheran	Methodist
An ordained, seminary-educated pastor whom you would share with one or more other congregations/parishes.*	65	56	57	55
An ordained, seminary-educated pastor who would work only part-time in your church while working part of full-time in another occupation.	17	36	33	33
A non-ordained person who has not had a formal seminary education, but has had training in pastoral leadership and is available to work full-time.	11	5	7	9
One or more lay persons of the congregation/parish who are trained and authorized to fulfill most or all pastoral roles on a part-time basis	8	4	4	3
	101	101	101	100

*The Protestant wording is shown here. In the Catholic questionnaire the word "priest" was used in place of "seminary educated, ordained pastor."

If No Full-Time Clergy Is Available

A main reason for doing the present research was the problem of what to do if a full-time clergy is not available for a parish. Many Protestant parishes are too small to afford one, and the Catholic Church has a priest shortage. What should be done?

Our questionnaire included several approaches to the problem. Table 5.8 shows the results on the most direct question. The four responses are arranged in the order of their popularity among the respondents (in the questionnaire they were in a different order). One conclusion is loud and clear: *the lay leaders prefer ordained over non-ordained leadership.* The most-selected choices involve ordained ministers, and the two choices utilizing non-ordained leaders are far behind.

The table contains another conclusion: *clergy who spend all their time working in religion are preferred* over those who are part-time in church work and part-time in another occupation. The two conclusions have an affinity, in that clergy are preferred over non-clergy, and full-time are preferred over part-time (who are probably seen as "part-clergy").

We looked for differences in attitudes according to parish staffing patterns, but none appeared. Laity in all sizes of parishes have similar views on these questions.

A second question was asked on the same topic. It described "tent-making" ministries and asked the lay leaders to evaluate them. See Table 5.9. (This question was not included in the Catholic questionnaire, since the concept of tent-making ministries is not widely known among Catholics and is not pertinent for the Catholic institutional problems.)

The evaluations of tent-making ministries are mixed, but in general rather unfavorable. As the table shows, attitudes vary widely, but the number who have a negative view ("regrettable") outweigh those with a positive view ("exciting" or "should be encouraged"). All the denominations agree. And when we looked

Table 5.9
Evaluation of Tent-Making Ministries (Percent)

How do you feel about the use in parish or congregation leadership of "tent-making" ministries (that is, ordained or lay professional ministers whose principal income derives from non-church sources)? Percentages:

	Catholic	Episcopal	Lutheran	Methodist
1. An exciting development	(not asked)	7	4	4
2. Should be encouraged in some cases but not generally		32	24	26
3. Appropriate for lay professionals but not for ordained persons		28	28	32
4. A regrettable but financially necessary development		17	22	24
5. A regrettable development that should be stopped		16	23	14
		100	101	100

at parish size, we found that laity from large or small parishes also agree.

The impending priest shortage in the Catholic Church is apparently evoking some strong feelings, as evidenced by the numerous spontaneous comments written on the questionnaires by Catholics. Many of the lay leaders said they favored married priests or women priests. For example, a Catholic from Washington:

I believe that our whole theology and practice of deciding who has received a call from God to the priesthood needs to be re-thought. The very idea that God would not call a leader forth from a body of believers as large as most Catholic parishes is hard to imagine. Yet we have a severe priest shortage. It seems to me we are not accepting the people he has called (married men and women—married or not).

A Catholic from Texas:

With the shortage of priests in our diocese I think it's vital that we start using our laicized inactive priests—those inactive who are in good standing with the church and want to become more of a help to their active brothers in Christ.

Yet another from Washington:

I have a concern not addressed in this questionnaire. How do we foster vocations to the priesthood? Is not the center of our Catholic religion the Eucharist and is it not our belief that the ordained priest is given the power, the authority, to consecrate, to celebrate this mysterious presence of God with us? Without the Eucharist do we have a Catholic Church, or do we have a sophisticated social agency? I personally need a priest (duly ordained) (married, man or woman) who represents Christ, who stands in union with the entire church, yet also stands ready to experience God. He/She does more than hold a community together. It is in the sharing of the Eucharist that this community is transformed beyond an earthly club to an experience of God's life. We need priests!

Attitude Differences by Sex, Education, and Region

It is important to know if these attitudes of the elected lay leaders vary along sex, education, or regional lines. If women have different attitudes than men, how? If the more educated have different views than the less educated, how? Since educational standards are gradually rising in the United States, persons with higher levels of education in 1987 are some indication of the future.

In general, the sex differences in our survey were smaller than education differences. The sex differences were only twofold. First, in all the denominations the women believed more than the men that "other staff" in parishes *should* have a great influence on decision-making. Why is this? One guess: perhaps the women leaders are in closer touch with parish staff persons than the men.

Second, on several measures Catholic women were less concerned about having ordained priests carry out certain leadership tasks. They had less of a preference than Catholic men that priests lead pastoral prayers and teach confirmation classes or new member classes. If a full-time priest could not be obtained, the Catholic women were disproportionately open to non-ordained parish leadership.

Turning to education differences, we find that in general the more educated respondents made weaker distinctions between clergy and laity. In all the denominations, the more educated respondents had less of a preference than the less educated that (a) an ordained clergy counsel them about problems, (b) an ordained clergy visit them in the hospital, and (c) an ordained clergy manage the organizational affairs of the parish. Also the more educated respondents were less concerned than others that adding paid lay professionals would undermine the prestige and authority of the pastor, or that it would cause the number of volunteers to drop. In all four denominations the *less* educated persons disproportionately believed that "the average lay person in this parish responds better to the leadership of someone who is ordained."

In the Protestant denominations there were two additional findings. One was that the respondents with less education rated the diocese, synod, or conference as having a higher level of influence on parish decision-making. Also they believed it *should* have a higher level of influence.

The overall picture is that the more educated lay leaders were less awed by ordained clergy, they were more ready to add lay professionals to church staffs, and they were more resistant to diocesan or synod influence on their parish.

Regional differences were scrutinized as much as possible, given the limitations of the study. We divided the questionnaires into three regions, as noted earlier—Northeast, Southeast, and West. The main regional differences occurred among Catholics. The respondents from the West were less concerned about the priest-laity distinction and ordination. The Catholics in the West disproportionately (a) had less preference for priests in giving sermons, counseling individuals, visiting someone in the hospital, and managing organizational affairs; (b) evidenced lower overall satisfaction with parish leadership; (c) disbelieved that adding paid lay professionals would undermine the pastor or cause volunteering to drop; and (d) believed that many ministerial tasks could be done well by competent lay leaders. If faced with the loss of a full-time priest, the Catholics in the West were less insistent that their parish leader be a priest rather than a lay person. (Already we have noted that the Catholic respondents from the West had higher educational levels than those from the other regions.)

In all the Protestant denominations there was a similar kind of pattern, but much weaker. Persons from the West worried less that introducing paid lay professionals would undermine pastoral influence and cause volunteering to drop off. The pattern is subtle, not as pronounced as among Catholics.

Summary

We have called attention to a large number of specific findings, of which a few seem important enough to be repeated. We were very interested to see if satisfaction and morale of laity depend on level of clergy staffing, and we found that it does only for Methodists. Elsewhere it does not; the laity in multiple-clergy parishes or part-time-clergy parishes were similar in morale and satisfaction. A lot depends on the individual clergy, apparently more than on the level of staffing.

There is no evidence for the argument that the more the paid staff, the less the lay involvement in the parish; on the contrary the opposite was true in three of the denominations.

Catholic parishes reported a bit lower levels of lay involvement and less participation of members in decision-making. Also the Catholics gave their staffs a bit lower ratings than did the other denominations. The Lutherans gave their staffs the highest ratings.

Laity have definite ideas about what leadership tasks are important. Preaching, worship, religious education, and pastoral care are foremost. Satisfaction with how these tasks are carried out varies from high to low, and the most notable finding was the rather low effectiveness rating on "deepening parishioners' spiritual life."

Everyone agrees that people respond better to ordained ministers than to lay ministers, and everyone agrees in desiring full-time clergy in their parishes, if possible.

The prospect of tent-making ministries does not appeal widely. If part-time clergy are inevitable, people prefer that they be full-time in religious work of some kind or other, not part-time in secular employment.

Finally, the more educated laity make smaller distinctions between ordained and non-ordained leadership, and they are more
open to increased laity on staffs. The same statement is true in
the Western part of the United States, where the people are less
concerned about clergy-laity distinctions—especially Catholics.

Part Four

Conclusions and Commentaries

6.

Implications and Concluding Reflections

Our purpose in this book has been to answer two basic questions about possible patterns of parish leadership for Roman Catholics and Protestants. The first question was about the financial cost of the main options. The second was about their perceived effectiveness. There are, of course, numerous other issues to be considered as church leaders plan the future, especially ecclesiological factors. But we believe that reliable information on costs and lay attitudes is needed, and recently it has been in short supply.

111

Here in the final chapter we will not summarize our research findings. Instead we will highlight several of our discoveries and comment on their implications.

Compensation: What Does Parish Leadership Cost?

We have attempted to provide careful estimates of the costs of parish leadership, lay and ordained, in the four communions. We have seen that the average cash salaries of full-time Protestant clergy vary only slightly among the three Protestant denominations. When we add other compensation, however, Episcopal clergy receive somewhat more than their Lutheran and Methodist counterparts. Catholic priests, on the other hand, are paid quite a bit less, both in cash and total compensation. We were surprised at the magnitude of the difference. We knew that the cash salary of priests was considerably lower, but we had expected that "perks" such as rectories, housekeepers, food allowances, and travel would be higher for priests, making the total compensation package more similar to Protestant ministers. But the total Catholic figures were lower.

To put these salaries into broader perspective, we can compare them with the compensation of other professionals, especially in professions resembling the clergy in education and responsibility. For secondary school teachers the average 1985 cash salary was $24,300; for college professors (all ranks and disciplines), it was $33,400. Social workers with a Master's degree earned $27,700.[1] Thus the Protestant clergy in our study have cash salaries only slightly lower than secondary school teachers and social workers, and moderately lower than college professors. But when the *total compensation* is considered, the Protestant ministers do relatively better. Of course, were we able to ascertain the total compensation of the other professionals, their figures would also be higher by maybe 10 or 20 percent. In contrast, Catholic priests receive considerably less compensation than the other professionals.

How much should clergy be compensated? How important is compensation in a person's choice of a profession? Would either the quantity or quality of clergy improve if they were better paid? These questions remain unanswered. We recognize that persons do not typically choose to pursue ordained or lay professional ministry with salary as a primary consideration. At the same time, it would surprise us if compensation did not play some role in decisions to enter the ministry or stay in it.

Cost of Lay Professionals

Issues of equitable compensation are important when we consider our findings for lay professionals, especially Catholic women religious. As we have seen, full-time lay professionals and Catholic women religious receive much lower compensation than ordained clergy, Catholic or Protestant. We were not surprised to find that Protestant lay professionals are, on average, less well compensated than ordained clergy. However, some Catholics seem to believe that priests cost less than lay professionals, and our findings will be important news to them. A priest's monthly *salary* is a good bit lower than a lay professional's, but the hidden benefits for priests are expensive, raising their total compensation above that of lay leaders. We believe that Catholics can afford the cost of lay professional leaders as an alternative to having parishes staffed only with priests. This is not to say that the laity are eager to hire laypersons; on the contrary, Catholic laity, like Protestant laity, much prefer ordained clergy as leaders.

The salaries of lay professionals, both Protestant and Catholic, seem low. They are low, for example, compared with the cash salaries of school teachers or social workers. Some of this difference is a result of unevenness in the qualifications of parish lay professionals. Yet it is safe to say that lay professionals in churches receive salaries lower than most professions with the same level of education. This is partly a product of the attractiveness of the jobs and hence the abundance of persons wanting to fill them. The social and spiritual rewards of parish ministry are such that many capable people are willing to do them for less than similar secular jobs. This keeps wages low. As a result most lay ministers are not persons providing the primary income for middle-class households. Rather, most are young adults, retirees, or persons whose spouses earn a good living. At present the majority are women.

Catholic religious women receive compensations which are indefensibly low. Our data show that they are paid substantially less than priests and other full-time lay professionals, regardless of their educational and professional qualifications. The low compensation of sisters generally, whether in parish ministry or other forms of church service, has become an embarrassment to many in the church, and positive steps are being taken today in some places.

Implications for Small Protestant Churches

A central concern behind this research was whether parishes with or without full-time ordained clergy differ in how well they serve the faithful. Are parishes without clergy a less supportive institutional arrangement and hence a poor second choice for structuring the Christian community? And similarly, do large and small parishes differ in their effectiveness? Our findings from lay leaders in parishes with and without full-time clergy revealed no clear differences. Parish morale is similar whether or not a full-time clergy is present. Only among Methodists did we find a pattern—that parishes with full-time ministers had higher morale and better lay participation, and, in addition, parishes with multiple staff had even higher morale. But in general, people apparently get used to what they have. No denomination should expect an overall change in parish morale if the level of staffing moves up or down. At most there would be a short-term change during the transition.

But there *is* a financial implication. Small parishes are more expensive per member. And the members give more. The cost of religious leadership per household is much higher in small parishes, regardless of denomination. This may tell us that the small parishes mean more to their members, on the average, than large parishes do. Possibly the small parishes are experienced as more supportive.

If, for a moment, we look at both Protestant and Catholic parishes, we see the same pattern writ large. The Catholic parishes are almost ten times as big, on average, as the Protestant, and their financial cost per household is very much lower. Also the number of members per clergy is vastly higher. When we compare large and small Catholic parishes, we find no difference in parish morale as reported by lay leaders. When we compare Catholic and Protestant parishes, we find that satisfaction with parish leadership *is* a bit lower for the Catholics than for the Protestants. Whether this is attributable to the large size of Catholic parishes is unclear; it may result from some other Catholic-Protestant difference.

Our compensation data sheds light on another issue—subsidies. The payment of subsidies in Protestant denominations is a way of enabling small parishes to afford a full-time clergy, whether singly or in some combination with another parish. This practice has much to commend it in certain situations: for example, in new congregations, in older small congregations located in rapidly-growing areas, or in some other special circumstance warranting assistance. As a general policy, however, the practice of subsidizing small congregations has come under increasing criticism. Not only do subsidies compete with other denominational priorities for scarce resources (Schaller, 1987), but they also often produce situations of unhealthy dependence of the local church on the denomination, and this may breed resentment. Subsidies were not a primary concern of our research, but our findings do have implications regarding them.

In congregations with less than one full-time ordained pastor, we were able to break our sample into two groups: one which included pastors who receive all of their income from church sources, the other with pastors who receive only part of their income from the parish. The former included a number of clergy in yoked parishes whose salary from the yoked congregations was subsidized by the denomination. The latter group included part-time pastors, either retired or in some dual-role capacity, who receive only part of their income from church sources. Their salaries were not subsidized by the denomination. In our data these two groups were small, making it risky to make too much of differences between them. With this caution, however, recall that the first group of pastors averaged $29,000 to $31,500 in total compensation; the latter group received between $10,000 and $12,000, about one-third as much. We cannot say whether the congregations in the first group are receiving more or better quality service. But we can say that the differences in total compensation, taken by themselves, make a strong financial case against the use of subsidies in these situations. A similar point is forcefully made by an Episcopal church consultant, Charles R. Wilson (1988:4), who tracked ten small Episcopal congregations in a single diocese over a 13-year period. During this time the congregations received approximately one million dollars in diocesan subsidies for clergy support. Wilson concludes:

> In 13 years of strategizing, an investment of one million dollars, plus immeasurable hours of time and miscellaneous expense, here's the result: church growth, zero; increased fiscal self-sufficiency, zero; clergy job satisfaction, probably close to zero; membership, settled into a permanent dependency mode.

Lay Attitudes About Ordained and Non-Ordained Ministers

Our survey of lay attitudes also has some important findings for church leaders to ponder.

As we have seen, Catholics, like Protestants, prefer ordained over lay leadership. While their preference for priests in some tasks of ministry is not so strong as that of Protestant laity, Catholics clearly would rather have the leadership of priests. One reason is apparently that their experience with lay ministers has been uneven; in the past not all lay leaders have proven capable and effective. Priestly ordination, by contrast, requires lengthy training and preparation, producing a general expectation among laity that priests will be dedicated and competent. The preference for priests is not felt equally by all Catholics; in particular, the better-educated Catholics in our survey were less concerned to have priests in various roles.

The impending priest shortage is a topic about which strong feelings were voiced by Catholic laity. They don't like it. Rather than suffer a loss of ordained priests to serve their parishes, the laity would prefer to have married priests or women priests. The option of having lay leaders for their parishes is not quite as acceptable. We are led to believe that Catholics would increase their financial giving if it would get them the parish leadership they want; if married priests were permitted, most laity would be ready to raise their contributions to have them.

Catholics indicate more dissatisfaction than Protestants with the current performance of their clergy. We are not sure why this is the case; all we can do is speculate. It may be that the Catholic theology of ordained ministry, which places heavy emphasis on the sacramental role of the priest, leads to an under-emphasis on other ministerial skills when priests are trained. Although there have been many changes in Catholic seminary education since Vatican II, the traditional Tridentine spiritual emphasis in priestly formation is still dominant. Thus, competence in preaching, teaching, parish administration and the like may have received less emphasis. (A related factor, incidentally, may also lie behind the somewhat more negative evaluation of priestly effectiveness by Episcopal lay leaders. Episcopalians are like Catholics in emphasizing the sacramental dimensions of the clergy role.) Or possibly the explanation of the lower effectiveness ratings of priests by Catholics may lie in the size of Catholic parishes; they are typically much larger than Protestant congregations, and, because of the priest shortage, sometimes understaffed. Thus Catholic laity may feel they are not getting adequate pastoral services. Whatever the reason, there is a noticeable amount of dissatisfaction with priestly effectiveness.

Among both Catholic and Protestant lay leaders we found broad dissatisfaction with the ability of the parish leadership to help deepen parishioners' spiritual lives. The laity want improved spiritual lives but are dissatisfied with the help they are getting from their churches. This discontent is strong and it is present in all four denominations. It is a principal finding of the study, which needs to be disseminated and analyzed further. This finding showed up unexpectedly in our lay leaders' ratings of leadership; it was not something we set out to study directly. But the lay leaders sent us a conspicuous signal.

When we turn to the views of Protestants about ordained and non-ordained ministers, we find mixed feelings. Lay leaders from small churches, while preferring full-time leadership, are generally realistic enough to know that it is seldom attainable. Thus, they do not believe that parish morale would suffer greatly if they had no full-time leadership. But they do strongly prefer *ordained* over lay leadership, and they also strongly prefer having an ordained clergyperson who is employed *full-time in religious work*. There is little sympathy for dual-role or tent-making styles of ministry in which the minister works part- or full-time in a secular occupation.

On the positive side there is an openness of small church leadership to sharing a pastor with another congregation or church-related job, or participating in a cluster arrangement. This openness is helpful to denominational leaders as they consider options for leadership in small congregations. It is also encouraging to lay leaders in congregations that are forced by circumstances to move from full- to part-time pastoral leadership. Shared or part-time clergy leadership does not mean "the end of the world" for their parish.

Less positive, however, are lay attitudes toward a tent-making minister or toward the use of indigenous lay leadership—two options that writers about small congregations often highly recommend. We have noted the already widespread use of tent-making ministries reported in a 1974 survey; it remains common today. Also there are growing numbers of advocates for the use of indigenous trained lay leadership, especially among Episcopalians, and a series of successful experiments has been described (Mathieson, 1979). The idea has been strongly endorsed within the Church of England, which is facing an acute priest shortage (Russell, 1980; Tiller, 1983). We believe that both of these options—tent-making clergy and indigenous lay professionals—are important for providing leadership in small congregations. While each has its limitations,[2] each also has great strengths, not as a "last ditch" means of providing pastoral care, but as a way of providing vital and effective parish leadership. It is clearly more defensible in financial terms to help small congregations find able leaders whom they can afford than to strain scarce congregational resources or resort to denominational subsidies. It also does little for the morale of ordained clergy to be subsidized for full-time ministry in one or more small congregations which do not offer a full workload.

In the face of widely-heard arguments for increasing tent-making ministries and the use of indigenous lay leadership, we would caution denominational leaders to be mindful of the rather strong negative attitudes of our lay leaders towards them—or to put the lay attitudes more positively, their strong preference for ordained leadership that is full-time in religious work. No matter that both tent-making and indigenous lay leadership have long pedigrees, stretching back to the earliest days of the church; the image of a successful church as one with full-time ordained leadership is widely accepted as normative by a majority of laity. In fact, most clergy and denominational leaders probably hold it as well. Our data imply that if either tent-making clergy or lay professionals are to find wide acceptance in small congregations, an educational effort will be needed to change perceptions and break the grip of this image of a successful church. It will also need to be backed up with clergy who can function effectively in dual roles or with laity who are adequately trained.

If lay attitudes towards tent-making clergy and lay professionals are rather negative, they are favorable towards options that involve full-time clergy, whether through yoking or other patterns. The latter include such strategies as clustering or group ministries noted in Chapter 1. Advocates for small congregations have often expressed doubts about such options: yoking sometimes creates tensions for clergy and laity as the congregations try to adjudicate disputes over loyalties, schedules and time commitments. Also clustering and group ministries sometimes appear to introduce into small parishes the criteria of effectiveness and success drawn from large parishes, and this violates the family-like intimacy which is a hallmark of small congregations (Carroll, 1977; Dudley, 1978; Walrath, 1983). While we believe that there is some justification for these criticisms, we simply note again that lay leaders seem to favor these options more than use of tent-making clergy or lay professionals. We suspect that the key issue is less the particular institutional arrangement than the preference for full-time clergy.

The lay attitudes regarding power and influence in parish life tell us that in all the denominations the laity favor more democracy and broad participation. The preference for ordained leaders in parishes does not mean that laity prefer clergy to rule over them. Rather, in all the denominations, we found a deep-set assumption that the total lay membership is capable of greater participation in parish decision-making than it exercises at present, and having it would be legitimate.

Some Implications for Theological Education

Our findings raise several questions related to theological education. The education of lay professionals is a major need for both Catholics and Protestants, but especially for Catholics for whom the problem is most immediately pressing. As we have noted, all signs point to the increased use of Catholic lay professionals as the principal strategy for meeting the priest shortage. Also for Protestants it has the potential of being important for meeting the needs of small parishes. In both traditions, this strategy will be effective only if the lay professionals are adequately trained so they can minister effectively.

Currently, many aspiring Catholic lay ministers are enrolled in programs leading to a Master of Arts degree, with a focus in some aspect of pastoral ministry, or to a Master of Divinity degree. Many of these programs exist in Catholic seminaries. It seems to us that these seminary programs provide both aspiring priests and lay professionals a good opportunity to learn to work together and develop appreciation for each other's complementary roles in ministry. Recall that a number of lay professionals complained that priests often lacked such appreciation, and this led to difficult staff relationships.

Protestant laity commonly study in seminary programs which also prepare persons for ordination. Most, however, choose not to enter such programs if they themselves are not seeking ordination. Instead they are more likely to enroll in M.A.

programs providing basic theological and professional preparation for ministerial work, or they work for certification as lay professionals in various church-sponsored training programs. Many of these programs are designed to enable laity to study part-time while working full-time. Doing this appears to result in great variation in program content, length, depth, and (in our experience) quality. As we have seen, the fear of poor quality is a factor in lay leaders' rather negative assessment of the use of lay professionals. These hesitations will need to be calmed down if lay professionals are to become an acceptable option for serving small Protestant parishes. Lay training needs to be improved.

An understanding of the uniqueness of ministry in small congregations is needed by both Protestant seminarians preparing for ordination and Protestant lay professionals. Size makes for important differences in the way congregations function and in the kind of pastoral leadership they require, as a number of studies have emphasized (e.g., Dudley, 1978; Schaller, 1982, 1985; Rothauge, n.d.). Many observers have noted that most Protestant seminaries ignore these differences. It is fair to say that most fail to prepare students adequately for ministry in small congregations. Rather, the picture of viable and successful ministry that students receive is typically that of large congregations with considerably more programs and resources than exist in most parishes in their denomination. Yet most of these students will spend a part, if not all, of their careers as pastoral leaders in these small congregations in some capacity or other. Their ministry would be greatly enhanced by an appreciation of small congregations, of which there are so many.

In Conclusion: Some Personal Observations

We wish to conclude with a few personal observations. Readers may protest that we have already included a number of personal observations about various issues, and that is correct.

Here, however, we wish to emphasize our convictions about the importance of the church's ministry and how we hope our findings can help that ministry.

In the Introduction we called attention to the growing convergence in Catholic and Protestant views of ministry. The convergence is clear from both the new perspectives articulated in the Second Vatican Council and the 1982 World Council of Churches document, *Baptism, Eucharist, and Ministry.* Each strongly affirmed the view of ministry as the vocation of the whole people of God, both lay and ordained. Lay ministry takes several forms, but in this report we have looked mostly at one form—leadership in parishes by laity professionally trained for ministry. We have said very little about the ministry of lay Christians outside the parish in the many spheres of public and private life. Our lack of attention to the latter is not because we see it as unimportant. To the contrary, we believe that enabling Christians to fulfill their callings in the world is a fundamental aim of the church and a central task of professionally trained pastoral leaders. If we have focused on lay ministry in the parish, it is because we believe enriching parish life is necessary to empower the ministry of all God's people in the world. Lay parish ministry is needed to energize lay workplace ministry.

Our approach to the crises of Protestant and Catholic parish leadership has had a limited focus. We have looked primarily at financial costs, effectiveness, and acceptability of various possibilities in the future. Such information is essential for responsible decision-making, but these considerations are only a portion of those church leaders need to ponder. The total picture includes theological norms, the tradition of the churches, information about social and economic factors, and the experience of faithful Christians in many places. Our hope has been to add to the knowledge available.

Finally, we acknowledge our enthusiasm over the ecumenical character of this study. Our research is not the first to have crossed Catholic and Protestant lines, but it is one more sign that the different communities have much to teach each other when they focus on a central issue such as ministry. In carrying out this project, we have had to struggle to understand the different ways Catholics and Protestants express similar beliefs and practices, and the common words they use which actually signify real differences. But if our experience is an indication, there is much that Catholics and Protestants have to contribute to each other as all share a common faith and a common mission in the service of Jesus Christ.

Commentary: Challenges for the Church of Tomorrow

Most Reverend Thomas J. Murphy*

One of the realities in countless structures and organizations today is the recognition of a need to plan to address issues in the future. Such planning is also a part of the experience of the Church today. Within the Roman Catholic faith community, developmental planning for the future has become a priority at the parish and diocesan level in many parts of our country. We are asking the basic questions needed to plan for the future: Who are we? Where do we want to go? What are our priorities? What strategies do we employ to get there? What major resources do we commit to help make our plans a viable reality?

The publication of *Patterns of Parish Leadership* provides additional information for the planning process. It addresses the concrete issue of the financial resources needed to provide pastoral care for people, which has a special practical significance for Roman Catholics. The Church faces this issue in light of two realities: a dwindling number of priests and growth of the Catholic community in many parts of our country.

Facing the costs of professional parish leadership has an even greater imperative as the Church utilizes more and more the ministry of religious women and professionally trained lay mini-

*Thomas J. Murphy is Coadjutor Catholic Archbishop of Seattle.

sters. How does the Church fund this ministry in a way which is consistent with its own teaching regarding justice in wages and compensation for all people in the workplace? Financial support of ministers in the Church becomes even more challenging in light of the available data on the financial support of Catholics for ministry in the Church today in comparison with other faith traditions.

Within the Roman Catholic Church today, there is more than the practical issue of the costs of professional parish leadership. There is also the unique role and responsibility of the priest. It is a question of ministry. Roman Catholic theology does not see ministry in a univocal way or from an egalitarian point of view. Rather, it recognizes that only the ordained priest is able to celebrate the Eucharist, which is at the core of Roman Catholic worship. In light of the centrality of the Eucharist, it is quite understandable that lay leaders have a strong preference for the presence of ordained clergy to serve them, even on a part-time basis. When religious women or lay professionals assume the major responsibility for pastoral care in a parish community, more than education is needed, as the study indicates; there is a need to appreciate worship experiences other than Eucharist.

In preparing candidates for priesthood today, seminaries have been reminded that they must share with their future priests a clear view of the priesthood and the positive value of celibacy. Moreover, they are asked to understand the meaning of ministry which is today often spoken of only in generalized terms with emphasis on the common priesthood of all the faithful by reason of baptism. Priesthood candidates are also asked to recognize the pressure coming from the movement for the ordination of women.

While the Church deals with these issues in the formation and education of future priests, it is trying to respond to its basic mission of the pastoral care of its people. The present study reveals the existence of a significant number of religious women and lay professional ministers in Roman Catholic parishes. Yet, ways must be found to help parishioners recognize the need to provide such ministers with a just salary and benefits. Roman Catholics could learn much from stewardship programs in Protestant congregations, which would increase available funding for ministry.

The very structure of the Roman Catholic Church has encouraged some dioceses to ask for financial support from larger and more affluent parishes in order to provide for the financial support of lay ministers in smaller parishes and rural areas. Such "twinning" has helped to raise the consciousness of people in the broader Church community with regard to the increasing presence of non-ordained persons serving the Church today.

Patterns of Parish Leadership offers information on the concrete issues of funding people who serve within the Church today, ordained and non-ordained. Yet, there is the deeper theological issue regarding ministry in the Roman Catholic faith community. In addressing the concrete and theological issues, the Catholic faith community is offered a unique challenge.

In a recent publication from the Bishops' Committee on Priestly Life and Ministry of the National Conference of Catholic Bishops, entitled *A Shepherd's Care: Reflections on the Changing Role of Pastor,* there is an overview of the transformation which has taken place in pastoring over the past twenty years. It recognizes the changing roles, the changing relationships, and the changing environment in which the pastor shares his ministry. It acknowledges the different forms and styles of pastoring and the need for support systems to enhance his role and responsibility. Finally, it looks to the future by identifying trends within the Church and the challenges which these trends present to pastors, bishops, and the Christian community. It is interesting to note that these trends and challenges coincide with the questions raised in the present study concerning the costs of professional parish leadership.

The first trend is the changing profile of the American parish, which is characterized by new migrations of people, a changing ethnic make-up, and the increased presence of the elderly upon whom most parishes depend for financial support. The younger and more educated Catholics are developing what might be called a spirit of "selective compliance" in their response to Church teaching.

The challenges which come from this trend are obvious. The Church must respond creatively to the realities of both decline and growth in parish communities by becoming agents of change in social conditions as well as by seeking ways to encourage collaboration and increased participation of people in parish life. The changing ethnic character of American parishes will demand special sensitivity to language and cultural values as well as the encouragement of vocations to ministry from the respective ethnic communities.

Care for the elderly in parish communities has become a major issue of pastoral care. At the same time, there is the need to develop among the young a sense of parish affiliation and the support of the parish. Underlying these questions is the basic issue of evangelization. Parish communities are asked to shift from a service model of pastoring to an evangelizing or evangelical model. It is a question of maintenance or mission.

A second trend identified in *A Shepherd's Care* is the changing resources needed for parish staffing. The challenge is to adjust to these new resources. Yet, the immediate challenge for pastors is to reassess vocational recruitment for priesthood as a parish priority where the entire parish becomes involved in the discernment and encouragement of vocations.

There is the further challenge to forge new relationships between the pastor and deacons and lay ministers. Not only is the issue raised regarding the working relationship, but there are also the realities of compensation, job security, and the need to develop a spirituality for those in pastoral ministry.

A final trend concerns the changes taking place in parish structures and the status of parish communities. It is inevitable that some parishes will close; some will become missions; some will be consolidated with neighboring parishes. There will be the appointment of deacons, religious women, and professional lay ministers to leadership positions within parish communities which had previously enjoyed the presence of a resident pastor.

The challenge that comes from this trend is obvious, and it is recognized in the study. There will be feelings of abandonment on the part of pastors as they leave communities and know that no priest will replace them. There will be tremendous anger and frustration on the part of people themselves in the parish communities affected. If parishes must close, there will be the whole experience of death and dying, with the refusal to accept the reality that is obvious.

Church law envisions the restructuring of pastoral care in a parish or several parishes through the appointment of a deacon or another minister to offer immediate pastoral service. Yet, there is the danger that the priest-pastor will experience marginalization, finding himself peripheral to the day-to-day life of the clustered parish community, even as he meets the sacramental needs of the people.

The response to the issues raised in the present study and in *A Shepherd's Care* is found ultimately in the spirit and reality of collaboration. It is such collaboration which makes the issues raised in *Patterns of Parish Leadership* a challenge for the Church of tomorrow.

Commentary

Dolores R. Leckey*

Reading through this study reminds me of several gospel stories that recount the surprises the disciples encounter when they go fishing. The followers of Jesus seek only a few fish but unexpectedly find their nets filled with an abundance, more than they expected and probably more than they needed.

Patterns of Parish Leadership sets out to learn if the Catholic, Episcopal, Lutheran and Methodist Churches can afford lay ministers in leadership roles in their churches. The research net pulled in a wealth of unexpected information and raised some new questions. The original inquiry was motivated by some pressing needs in the denominations. In the Catholic Church, for example, the numbers of clergy are diminishing; in the other three denominations small parishes increasingly find it difficult to attract ordained leadership. Catholics have limited options for dealing with the situation since certain boundaries have been set: only celibate men may be priests. Deacons, who are clergy and who are typically married men, are numerous in the U.S. and could conceivably solve this problem. But the researchers maintain that deacons are rarely in full-time ministry, that for many people (particularly priests) the deacon's role is still unclear, and that the "diaconate seems to strengthen both clericalism and male models of leadership in a time when laymen and laywomen are rediscovering their roles in the ministry of the whole people of God" (ch. 1). It remains to be seen whether the

*Dolores Leckey is Executive Director, Secretariat for Laity and Family Life, National Conference of Catholic Bishops.

researchers are correct in their evaluation of the diaconate, but meanwhile what's a parish to do? Professional lay ministers are the most viable option, according to the researchers. But can the Church afford them? The study probed this question by examining the real costs of maintaining clergy in parishes. But when the authors went fishing for financial data they hauled in a collection of other information as well—important and surprising bits and pieces. It is the extras I wish to comment on.

(1) Catholic laity, like those in other denominations, clearly prefer to have priest-pastors. On the other hand, Catholics are willing to have professional lay ministers in other parish roles, for example, in religious education or in administration. What lies behind this dual message? Two significant experiences, I believe. One is the long and cherished tradition of being a sacramental church. The other is a developing history of lay people in parish ministry. The lay professional minister is not an unknown to Catholic communities. But neither is the distinction between priests and other ministers, which Catholics know and value.

(2) While Catholic lay leaders readily allow for the appropriate authority and influence of the priest-pastor in the parish, they seem to recognize that the parish pastoral council could and probably should play a more influential role in the life of the parish. If the parish council were to function as a vital consultative body, perhaps there would be a greater likelihood of more open discussion about the mission and ministry of the parish.

(3) Catholic financial support of parish ministers is significantly less than in the other denominations studied. What is the explanation? Is there a relationship between the Catholic giving pattern and spiritual vitality? Very likely.

(4) The unexpected finding in the study is that lay people in all four denominations yearn for greater spiritual development. This is worthy of extended comment.

Is in fact the typical parish able to help people cross over into the realm of the transcendent or to spiritual awareness? I think the answer is "yes," given certain conditions.

Prior to the 1987 Roman synod on the vocation and mission of the laity, the Bishops' Committee on the Laity conducted an extensive consultation in the United States; one of the areas of inquiry was the spiritual awareness, faith, and hope in the lives of ordinary people. In response to a column I wrote about encountering God in everyday life, hundreds of people wrote me accounts of the inner world of the spirit. Letters came from rural and urban settings, from people as old as ninety and as young as ten. Families and parishes were named as the two primary places for encountering God. As I study their stories I see five ways that parishes are now, or might be, helpful in people's spiritual quest.

(1) *Worship.* Lay people who participated in the pre-synod consultation are clear that they want and need good liturgy in order to grow spiritually. They view clergy and religious as spiritual leaders not merely in the sense of celebrating sacraments ritually, but in the sense of facilitating their prayer life. When we put this conviction together with the findings in *Patterns of Parish Leadership* we see the need for priest-pastors to reorder their priorities, particularly their time, so that through personal prayer and meditation they will be leaders of worship who contribute to the enrichment of community consciousness and the human instinct for God. As the pastoral leadership moves more deeply into the life of the Spirit, levels of trust and patterns of collaboration will surely develop, for to be in the Spirit of God is to live the theology of First Corinthians—a theology of shared ministry.

(2) *Spiritual direction.* The relationships of mentoring, guiding and befriending are all part of the Christian tradition. My own informal research indicates that laity today sense they need spiritual guides and/or spiritual friends if they are to grow

strong in the life of the Spirit. The parish is one place where those gifted as spiritual friends can be identified, called forth, trained perhaps, and encouraged to utilize their gifts on behalf of the larger community.

(3) *Dialogue.* Jesuit sociologist John Coleman believes that laity today need opportunities for "a new kind of talking"—what I would call dialogue. What we both mean is that spiritual vitality calls for small groups of Christians who will gather on a regular basis to explore the hope and the faith in their lives. It is such conversation, contends Coleman, that yields a true lay spirituality, rooted as it is in the everydayness of work and family, of civic culture and church culture. A pastoring style that enables small communities to gather and pray and dialogue about the connections between the inner life and the outer life of work, family and society is one that fosters a whole spirituality.

(4) *Education and support for ministry.* The lay persons wrote forthrightly about their ministry and service. Their testimony is that the practice of ecclesial ministry has the effect of sensitizing them to their secular responsibilities. A bank president wrote that since he's been a reader at Mass he thinks about his clients differently, and he attributes that to his immersion in the Scriptures. An extraordinary minister of the eucharist tells of how she looks at people in her neighborhood in a new way; being a minister has opened her eyes. The argument sometimes put forth that lay ministry is detracting from the laity's role in society is not supported by the available information. Rather, we see lay ministry serving as a means of spiritual formation.

(5) *Sabbath time.* Historically, one of the values of genuine sabbath has been to make present to us the truth about our dependence on God. This kind of awareness naturally leads one into a sense of transcendence, of contemplation and of play. Church may be one of the last institutions in society that can provide sabbath-time, that quality of being that appreciates what it is to be human and to be graced. If the parish were to help the

laity *to rest, to be* and *to play* as well as to minister and to work, then we might stay with the oftentimes arduous and demanding task of facing two worlds, the one within and the one all around us.

These suggestions for spiritual development in parishes depend not so much on technique as on attitude. The parish leadership (or somebody) will need to know the difference between successful efficiency and spiritual aliveness. (These need not be mutually exclusive, but they are surely not equivalent.) And then the leadership (or somebody) will have to care passionately about walking that spiritual path—and care enough to act. It seems to me that one test of the spiritual authenticity of any given parish is whether or not that parish is about the Church's mission to care for the world. Matthew 25 still stands as a major reference point to gauge whether we're fooling ourselves or not.

The next time the researchers go fishing, I for one hope they test these suggestions for parish spiritual development and look for the relationship between spirituality and the laity's willingness to care for the world. That could make for interesting fishing.

Commentary: What Are the Issues?

Lyle E. Schaller*

What do the people want?

What do the people need?

The tension generated by the conflicting responses to these two questions has engaged the attention of theologians, philosophers, ethicists and politicians for centuries.

The new study of the costs of parish leadership speaks to this distinction between what people want and what is realistic by introducing two additional factors. The first is the changing balance between the supply and demand of parish clergy, and the second is the total compensation required to provide a parish with a full-time resident minister.

This picture is further complicated by the fact that in the three Protestant denominations in the study the polity provides for a disproportionately large representation of people from smaller congregations at the annual convention of the regional judicatory. The policy-making processes are designed to give more votes to the smaller parishes. That built-in bias cannot help but influence the outcome of this debate between wants and needs.

*Lyle E. Schaller is Parish Consultant on the staff of the Yokefellow Institute and author of thirty books on churches.

Another perspective for looking at the data presented in this study is to turn to two sets of statistics.

The first is on the size of congregations. In 1975 a parish in the Lutheran Church in America needed to average 120 at worship to be listed among the larger one-half of all parishes in that denomination. By 1985 the number needed to be in the largest one-half had dropped to an average of 112 at Sunday morning worship.

Back in 1974 in the United Methodist Church a congregation had to average 119 at worship to rank among the largest one-fourth of all churches in the denomination. By 1986 that figure had dropped to 113.

If one argues that a congregation needs to average 120 at worship to justify and afford a full-time resident pastor, more than one-half of all Lutheran Church in America parishes cannot justify that arrangement. Fewer than one-fourth of all United Methodist congregations meet that criterion. What is even more significant is the diminishing proportion of churches that average 120 at worship.

If that cutoff is raised to a more defensible figure of 150 on average at worship, approximately 83 percent of all United Methodist congregations, 66 percent of all Lutheran Church in America congregations, 77 percent of all United Church of Christ congregations, 61 percent of all American Lutheran parishes, and 81 percent of all Southern Baptist churches did not meet that standard in 1985.

The second set of statistics is drawn from the heart of this report. The total compensation for the average Catholic priest exceeds $28,000 annually while for the three Protestant denominations studied, the total was approximately $40,000. By contrast, the average total cost to a parish for a full-time lay professional was approximately $20,000 a year.

For Catholics the four obvious pressures for employing a larger number of lay professionals are (a) the shortage of priests, (b) the lower cost of lay professionals, (c) the higher acceptance of lay professionals among people with a higher level of educational attainment—and an increasing proportion of Catholics now are college graduates, and (d) the increasing interest among women in becoming lay professionals.

Among Protestants the number-one pressure for greater use of lay professionals in the parish is that ordained clergy are being priced out of the ministerial marketplace. Two-thirds to four-fifths of all Protestant congregations cannot afford and justify a full-time resident pastor.

This leads us back to that pair of tension-producing questions. The present study makes it clear that the overwhelming majority of the laity want their congregation to be served by a full-time resident pastor. Should denominational leaders be sympathetic and responsive to that wish?

Or should these denominational leaders focus on the fact that the majority of parishes need to consider some other arrangement, even though it is not what the people want? Other research suggests that the use of bi-vocational ministers can have productive results. This study points out that the laity do not want it. Should it be advocated?

While it does not receive much space in this book, some of us will agree that the most significant discovery in this research is that among the laity the chief source of discontent is "the dissatisfaction with the ability of the parish leadership to help deepen parishioners' spiritual life." My research over the past quarter-century suggests that this is the most important single factor behind the migration of Catholics, Presbyterians, Methodists, Lutherans, and others to those large, rapidly growing, theologically conservative, and relatively new non-denominational churches all across the nation. The questionnaires in this study were completed by persons whose level of discontent had not reached a level that had caused them to leave. My own travels among the churches also suggest that when the parish leadership is able to satisfy this need for the spiritual growth of the members, it is relatively easy for a congregation averaging only sixty to ninety at worship to provide the financial support for a full-time resident pastor.

Perhaps the size of the congregation is not the key variable in determining the economic capability of a congregation to support a resident minister. This study makes it clear that the overwhelming majority of the laity want "our own pastor." The study also suggests that they want and need a minister who can help deepen the spiritual life of the parishioners. That need, rather than the request for denominational subsidies for clergy support in smaller parishes, may be the item that should be at the top of the agenda of denominational leaders.

This issue is more complicated for United Methodists than for other denominations. As this study points out, Methodists have a shortage of economically viable appointments and a surplus of clergy. With only 11,000 congregations that average one hundred or more at worship and nearly 22,000 parish pastors who are guaranteed appointments, some combination of subsidies, asking two or more congregations to share the time of one minister, and other arrangements are necessary, even though that clearly is not what the people want. The need to make the appointment system work has become a high priority.

Every once in a while a research report appears that not only plows new ground, but also sheds light and factual data on pressing contemporary issues. This report will be of tremendous help to those who must respond to a variety of wants and needs in ministerial placement.

Commentary

Loren B. Mead*

Most research is geared to discover answers to questions that are felt to be troublesome. Occasionally, when research is imaginative and open, it leads to deeper questions as well as answers to the questions that generated the research.

Rarely does research dramatically pose turning-point dilemmas so critical that one almost forgets the original question of the research.

This study, by looking at the prosaic issue of money and the "cost" of clergy, lifts up for those who choose to see it an immense issue that the Church has been avoiding for half a century: What happens when our paradigm of ministry dies?

Let me describe the paradigm whose death I see in the data gathered here. What I will say refers primarily to the "mainline denominations" described by McKinney and Roof in *American Mainline Religion* (Rutgers University Press, 1987).

The norm for ministry in this paradigm called for a skilled, theologically educated corps of more or less "professional" leaders deployed to local stations (parishes or congregations). The corps held control of crucial functions for the community. Within the more sacramental churches, those crucial functions usually related to ritual acts that were essential to the life of the institution. At its least mature, this led to the imputation of almost magical efficacy to the actions of leaders. In less sacramental

*Loren B. Mead is Executive Director of The Alban Institute, Inc., Washington, DC.

churches, the power of the office resided more in the obligation to interpret and proclaim the Word.

What was common to all the churches in this paradigm was the power of the ordained minister and the relative passivity of the non-ordained leader in matters of institutional life *and* self-conscious ministry. What the ordained leader did *was* ministry.

Local parishes and congregations were considered "good" and "successful" if they could accomplish several relatively simple things: support a full-time pastor, maintain a building, see to regular (usually at least weekly) services of worship, and manage their affairs so as not to overspend their funds, run afoul of the law or offend community standards. More central to the life of some congregations, but important to all, was the function of recruiting and nurturing an adequate number of new members.

Here I am not talking about the theological rationale for ministry or ecclesiology, but about rules so written into church custom (and usually in canons, church policy and rules of order) that the ordinary person in the pew "knows" it to be so.

Under that paradigm everybody "knows:" (1) The pastor is the minister (in spite of theologies of the priesthood of all believers). (2) Without a full-time pastor, the congregation is living in a second-best state, waiting until somehow a full-time person can be secured again. (3) No pastor worth her or his salt stays in a marginal or subsidized congregation, but seeks to move to a more "successful" one. (4) It is the congregation's job at least partly to work to see that the pastor and the pastor's interests are supported and that the pastor is kept satisfied by the challenge of the situations and the response of the people. (5) The key responsibility of the laity in strengthening ministry is to see that the congregation carries out its functions successfully (maintaining and paying for a full-time pastor and building, supporting regular worship, managing congregational affairs and recruiting new members).

I do not know when, if ever, people rationally accepted this as an adequate reflection of what they wanted ministry to be. Indeed, our rhetoric has generally been opposed to this as a model. But our behavior has supported it. The present research points to areas in which the paradigm still rules us.

For several generations there have been questions and challenges to this model.

The house-church movement was an attempt to discover a new model. Washington's Church of the Savior is one of the more successful attempts. The "Cluster Movement" of the 1960s and early 1970s attempted to develop groups of congregations exploring collective alternatives. Para-church organizations, from the Industrial Missions of the more liberal denominations to Youth for Christ, Fellowship of Christian Athletes, and Colson's Prison Ministry, tested other approaches. Today denominations continually experiment with "yoking," "merging," or other forms of linkages for congregations that cannot achieve the norm on their own. Judicatories develop elaborate mechanisms for taxing the "successful" congregations under this paradigm to pay for the congregations who cannot "make it" on their own.

None of the alternatives has seriously challenged the pastor-centered paradigm as the norm of ministry, although each has struggled to incarnate something new. The televangelists, on the other hand, have reinforced the old model, simply expanding the concept of the congregation technologically.

The research in this book tells us that this paradigm is dead. The economic basis for it no longer exists. The majority of Protestant congregations have fewer than 200 members. The cost of the current paradigm of ministry is prohibitive for many, perhaps most, congregations. Within the Catholic Church, demographics are different, but for other reasons it is less and less possible to provide each parish with a full-time priest.

In most of the denominations, temporary and experimental programs are being tried. "Non-stipendiary" clergy, "lay-clergy staff teams" (particularly in Catholic parishes), and "locally trained clergy" are ways some describe the attempts. A conference at Lincoln Cathedral, England, in 1988 brought together representatives from 40 Anglican dioceses around the world to discuss "non-stipendiary" and "tent-making" ministries. Participants were surprised at the extent and variety of experimentation going on only 24 years after the first official permission was given.

The disquieting evidence of the research in this book is that although the paradigm is dead, the ordinary church member is not interested in alternative forms.

The denominations, by treating this as a minor issue to be solved by better fund-raising or evangelism (sometimes betrayed by language: "recruiting more pledging units"), are supporting a fiction. They are colluding with those in the churches who look to recapturing a golden age that probably never existed. They are hiding their heads in the sand.

An enormous task lies ahead. This research opens the door to look through our theological statements and ecclesiological traditions to the economic and human realities that threaten our churches, and that lie beneath our institutional forms.

What are some of the specific questions we need to address?

• What *does* constitute effective ministry in a congregation?

• How do we develop norms that support a model of ministry based on that new understanding of effectiveness?

• What new roles are required of clergy and laity in a church committed to the primacy of the ministry of the laity?

• How do we train clergy as servants of the people?

• How do we train laity as ministers in the world?

• What institutional forms do we need to accomplish that?

• How do we learn to let go of the old paradigm, especially in those places where it remains economically possible?

• How do we build denominational structures that affirm a new paradigm?

• How do we train bishops and executives to support the new paradigm?

A new paradigm of ministry is struggling to be born, one that is based in commitment and witness of the individual Christian in the structures of the world. This research is about nothing less than that.

It tells us that a model we have loved and that has served us (and that we have known for some time to be theologically bankrupt), is breaking up and sinking under the weight of unsupportable economic realities. It tells us also that neither clergy nor laity are yet willing to face alternatives.

Research? Yes. But more important, I think this book is a call to leadership by those who care for the future of ministry and mission.

Appendix

Availability of Research Materials

Francis Scheets is keeping a supply of the research materials used in this study, including the financial report forms, the instruction handbook written for field coordinators, and both attitude questionnaires. Persons interested in them should contact him: Rev. Francis Kelly Scheets, OSC, Church Management Planning and Management Information, 19520 Darnestown Road, Beallsville, MD 20839. A copy of all materials has been deposited in Mullen Library, Catholic University of America and in Hartford Seminary Library, Hartford, Connecticut.

Table A.1
Average Size Parish by Household and Members, with Ratio of Laity to Clergy: by Denomination and Region of Country*

By Region & Denomination	Number Parishes (1)	Average Size Households (2)	Average Size Members (3)	Laity to Clergy Households (4)	Laity to Clergy Members (5)
NATIONAL AVERAGE:					
Roman Catholic	62	1,065	3,348	618	1,954
Episcopalian	46	246	476	162	313
Lutheran	46	183	411	133	304
Methodist	47	323	703	185	398
NORTHEAST:					
Roman Catholic	24	1,320	4,143	779	2,439
Episcopalian	18	223	485	158	346
Lutheran	18	180	423	141	330
Methodist	18	227	431	164	311
SOUTHEAST:					
Roman Catholic	22	934	3,125	484	1,631
Episcopalian	18	228	447	164	320
Lutheran	18	161	320	124	244
Methodist	18	278	758	209	569
WEST:					
Roman Catholic	16	897	2,636	653	1,917
Episcopalian	10	320	514	198	318
Lutheran	10	228	559	176	434
Methodist	11	547	1,041	280	528

* All data for this study is for 1986 fiscal year.

Table A.2
Average Size Parish by Household and Members with Ratio of Laity to Full-Time Clergy: by Type of Parish Staffing and Denomination

By Denomination & Parish Staffing	Parishes (1)	Clergy Full Time (2)	Clergy Part Time (3)	Average Size House-holds (4)	Average Size Members (5)	Laity to Clergy House-holds (6)	Laity to Clergy Members (7)
NATIONAL AVERAGE:							
Two or More Clergy	75	164	12	924	2,577	423	1,178
One Full-Time Clergy	82	82	13	339	958	339	958
No Full-Time Clergy	45	10	37	87	213	391	959
ROMAN CATHOLIC:							
Two or More Clergy	27	69	3	1,719	5,349	692	2,149
One Full-Time Clergy	25	25	8	692	2,272	691	2,232
No Full-Time Clergy	10	4	81	234	634	234	633
EPISCOPALIAN:							
Two or More Clergy	17	37	3	416	822	189	383
One Full-Time Clergy	19	19	2	202	376	202	376
No Full-Time Clergy	10	2	8	40	76	39	75
LUTHERAN:							
Two or More Clergy	14	27	1	338	734	176	383
One Full-Time Clergy	22	22	3	146	352	145	351
No Full-Time Clergy	10	2	9	47	91	46	90
METHODIST:							
Two or More Clergy	14	41	5	791	1,757	269	604
One Full-Time Clergy	22	16		155	313	213	430
No Full-Time Clergy	10	2	12	70	158	50	113

Table A.3

Full-Time Staff Per Parish Household: by Denomination and Type of Parish Staffing

By Denomination & Parish Staffing	Clergy Per Parish (1)	Lay Staff Per Parish		Full-Time Staff Per Parish (4)	Laity Per FTE Staff	
		Full-Time (2)	Part-Time (3)		Per Household (5)	Per Member (6)
NATIONAL AVERAGE:						
Two or More Clergy	2.2	1.6	1.5	3.8	243	678
One Full-Time Clergy	1.0	0.5	1.1	1.5	231	655
No Full-Time Clergy	0.2		0.3	0.3	326	799
ROMAN CATHOLIC:						
Two or More Clergy	2.6	2.6	1.6	5.1	334	1,039
One Full-Time Clergy	1.0	0.8	1.0	1.8	393	1,291
No Full-Time Clergy	1.0*	0.2	1.1	1.2	195	528
EPISCOPALIAN:						
Two or More Clergy	2.2	1.3	1.1	3.5	120	237
One Full-Time Clergy	1.0	0.5	0.6	1.5	137	255
No Full-Time Clergy	1.0*		0.2	1.0	40	76
LUTHERAN:						
Two or More Clergy	1.9	0.7	1.1	2.6	128	278
One Full-Time Clergy	1.0	0.3	1.6	1.3	111	267
No Full-Time Clergy	1.0*		0.1	1.0	47	91
METHODIST:						
Two or More Clergy	2.9	1.4	2.4	4.3	185	410
One Full-Time Clergy	0.7	0.1	0.9	0.9	180	362
No Full-Time Clergy	1.4*		0.1	1.4	50	113

*In these parishes full-time clergy were serving more than one parish.

Table A.4

Average Contributions Per Household and Per Member: Showing Relation to Expenses and Salaries

By Denomination & Parish Staffing	Average Contribution Per Household (1)	Per Member (2)	Expenses as Percent Contributions (3)	Salary as % of Contributions Dollars (4)*	Resources (5)**
BY DENOMINATION:					
Catholic	$278	$88	100%	30.8%	33.2%
Episcopalian	599	309	107	47.5	49.3
Lutheran	653	290	99	50.8	51.8
Methodist	553	254	98	38.3	41.1
BY PARISH STAFFING PATTERN:					
Two or More Clergy	$516	$185	101%	37.7%	39.8%
One Full-Time Clergy	507	179	109	39.5	42.5
No Full-Time Clergy	572	233	105	57.5	63.7
ROMAN CATHOLIC:					
Two or More Clergy	225	72	93	31.1	34.3
One Full-Time Clergy	248	75	107	25.2	28.4
No Full-Time Clergy	258	96	92	51.2	58.4

(Continued)

EPISCOPALIAN:				
Two or More Clergy	631	319	110	47.5	48.7
One Full-Time Clergy	542	291	103	45.0	48.1
No Full-Time Clergy	566	296	109	69.5	73.2
LUTHERAN:				
Two or More Clergy	658	303	95	46.7	47.2
One Full-Time Clergy	665	276	105	55.9	57.3
No Full-Time Clergy	525	271	111	54.5	57.2
METHODIST:				
Two or More Clergy	573	258	98	36.0	38.1
One Full-Time Clergy	504	251	94	42.3	46.6
No Full-Time Clergy	467	207	102	61.9	70.9

*Column 4 includes salary, allowances, and benefits.

**Column 5 includes salary, allowances, benefits and rental value of parish owned house.

Table A.5

Full-Time Clergy: Adjusted Average Total Compensation, Allowances, and Benefits, by Region and Denomination

By Region & Denomination	Number Persons	Total Compen- sation	Dollar Income	Housing/ Rent	Allowances + Travel Education		Benefits + Retirement Health SECA/ WC		
	(1)	(2)	(3)	(4)	(5)	(6)	(7)	(8)	(9)
NATIONAL AVERAGE: (Adjusted)*									
Catholic	98	$26,184	$7,472	$13,176	$3,121	$531	$999	$1,381	$399
Episcopalian	58	41,029	21,761	9,097	2,932	598	4,609	2,824	1,799
Lutheran	51	39,059	21,688	7,474	3,000	544	3,229	1,649	1,872
Methodist	59	35,308	20,833	8,190	2,822	473	3,018	1,444	1,274
Average	266	33,913	16,277	10,087	2,990	535	2,662	1,761	1,181
WESTERN STATES: (Adjusted)*									
Catholic	19	30,662	10,109	15,754	2,302	642	740	1,289	51
Episcopalian	16	40,524	20,341	2,516	2,443	536	5,147	2,922	--
Lutheran	12	38,055	20,247	7,401	2,930	613	3,552	1,346	2,374
Methodist	22	35,790	21,909	8,262	1,690	420	1,599	1,200	--
Average	69	35,870	18,007	8,843	2,249	541	2,525	1,649	427

(Continued)

NORTHEAST STATES: (Adjusted)*

Catholic	37	26,070	7,745	12,905	2,455	557	1,041	1,560	114
Episcopalian	19	46,501	20,739	11,840	2,801	304	5,293	1,898	1,193
Lutheran	20	35,534	18,388	8,287	2,710	328	2,565	1,244	718
Methodist	19	20,965	12,014	5,763	1,129	63	1,443	791	–
Average	95	31,128	13,438	10,291	2,313	359	2,293	1,407	434

SOUTHEAST STATES: (Adjusted):*

Catholic	42	23,681	6,012	11,864	3,302	364	671	1,307	371
Episcopalian	23	40,424	24,440	1,020	2,503	432	4,292	1,424	984
Lutheran	19	27,051	14,490	5,716	2,107	283	1,905	834	1,140
Methodist	18	20,844	11,099	4,339	1,796	286	2,361	506	425
Average	102	27,583	12,644	6,946	2,633	351	2,016	1,104	662

* Adjusted by parish staffing patterns for national & regional data

+ For those receiving allowances and/or social security.

Table A.6

Full-Time Clergy: Compensation Per Household, Housing, and Percent Receiving Allowances and Social Security: by Region and Denomination

By Region & Denomination	Compensation Per Household (1)	Housing*		Unadjusted Percent Receiving				
		Utilities/ Other (2)	Comparable Rent (3)	Allowances +			Education (7)	Benefits + SECA/WC (8)
				Utilities (4)	Rent (5)	Travel (6)		
NATIONAL AVERAGE: (Adjusted)*								
Catholic	$40	$8,536	$4,763	100%	96%	85%	100%	17%
Episcopal	241	8,697	8,078	90	19	74	72	36
Lutheran	382	7,580	8,589	88	8	92	84	47
Methodist	282	4,451	5,874	90	44	78	68	8
Average:	203	7,482	6,466	–	–	–	–	–
WESTERN STATES: (Adjusted)*								
Catholic	45	9,785	6,186	78	76	78	78	4
Episcopalian	241	10,131	4,144	61	10	68	78	–
Lutheran	292	8,603	1,232	67	10	76	51	39
Methodist	311	5,343	3,188	97	64	91	65	–
Average:	218	8,243	3,895	–	–	–	–	–

(Continued)

NORTHEAST STATES: (Adjusted)*

Catholic	36	8,617	4,288	70	70	54	70	1
Episcopalian	266	6,690	10,245	55	25	42	29	25
Lutheran	296	6,766	3,088	67	10	62	65	17
Methodist	111	2,251	4,886	50	44	32	43	—
Average:	152	6,569	5,346	—	—	—	—	—

SOUTHEAST STATES: (Adjusted)*

Catholic	68	7,582	4,563	70	68	62	70	25
Episcopalian	419	6,141	468	55	9	48	37	38
Lutheran	255	5,452	1,320	50	3	47	29	34
Methodist	96	3,018	1,804	55	26	55	33	17
Average:	187	6,055	2,549	—	—	—	—	—

* Adjusted by Parish Staffing Patterns for National & Regional Data

+ Unadjusted study data for those receiving allowances and/or social security. (See Table A.8)

Table A.7

Full-Time Clergy: Unadjusted Average Total Compensation, Allowance, and Benefits, by Denomination and Parish Staffing Pattern

By Parish Staffing	Number Persons	Total Compensation	Dollar Income	Housing/ Rent	Allowances* Travel	Allowances* Education	Benefits* Retirement	Benefits* Health	Benefits* SECA/ WC
	(1)	(2)	(3)	(4)	(5)	(6)	(7)	(8)	(9)
ROMAN CATHOLIC: (Unadjusted)*									
Two or More Clergy	69	$25,041	$7,243	$12,103	$3,410	$498	$1,026	1,332	$481
One Full-Time Clergy	25	28,201	7,917	14,903	2,887	584	998	1,410	311
Full-Time Clergy	4	19,464	5,748	8,368	2,346	375	747	1,612	370
	98								
EPISCOPALIAN (Unadjusted)									
Two or More Clergy	37	48,707	23,908	11,224	3,443	1,063	6,429	3,083	2,429
One Full-Time Clergy	19	43,672	21,473	10,616	2,726	650	5,304	2,957	2,410
No Full-Time Clergy	2	30,995	20,937	4,800	3,000	200	2,100	2,400	216
	58								
LUTHERAN: (Unadjusted)									
Two or More Clergy	27	40,094	21,691	7,903	2,973	636	3,745	1,549	2,188
One Full-Time Clergy	22	42,795	22,725	9,361	3,169	569	4,275	1,572	2,464
No Full-Time Clergy	2	28,976	19,398	2,550	2,677	325	--	2,000	--
	51								

(Continued)

METHODIST: (Unadjusted)

Two or More Clergy	41	39,977	23,154	9,754	2,843	575	3,440	1,676	3,190
One Full-Time Clergy	16	37,630	20,887	9,209	2,609	552	3,898	1,516	1,957
No Full-Time Clergy	2	31,636	19,961	6,750	3,000	369	2,106	1,300	--
	59								

* Unadjusted study data: For those receiving allowances and/or benefits.

Table A.8

Full-Time Compensation Per Household, Housing, and Percent Receiving Allowances and Social Security: by Denomination and Parish Staffing Patterns

By Parish Staffing & Denomination	Compensation Per Household (1)	Housing*		Unadjusted Percent Receiving*				
		Utilities/ Other (2)	Comparable Rent (3)	Allowances				Benefits
				Utilities (4)	Rent (5)	Travel (6)	Education (7)	SECA/WC (8)
ROMAN CATHOLIC: (Unadjusted)								
Two or More Clergy	$ 37	$8,113	$4,236	100 %	94 %	86 %	100%	20%
One Full-Time Clergy	41	9,522	5,381	100	100	80	100	4
No Full-Time Clergy	141	3,898	4,470	100	100	100	100	50
EPISCOPALIAN: (Unadjusted)								
Two or More Clergy	255	10,803	11,760	89	14	76	76	38
One Full-Time Clergy	216	7,526	11,040	95	32	68	68	32
No Full-Time Clergy	1,590	9,600	--	50	--	100	50	50
LUTHERAN: (Unadjusted)								
Two or More Clergy	229	9,062	14,000	81	4	93	89	44
One Full-Time Clergy	293	8,654	8,067	95	14	91	82	55
No Full-Time Clergy	852	2,550	--	100	--	100	50	--
METHODIST: (Unadjusted)								
Two or More Clergy	148	7,837	8,974	85	34	76	66	7
One Full-Time Clergy	176	4,909	6,880	100	63	81	75	13
No Full-Time Clergy	422	2,850	3,900	100	100	100	50	--

* Unadjusted study data for those receiving housing, allowances and/or benefits.

Table A.9

Pastoral Support Programs by Diocese, Synod, or Conference Per Active Clergy

| By Level of Denominational Authority | Pastoral Support Programs | | | | | | Total Support Cost Per Clergy (7) | Seminary Theological Education (8) |
| | Personal Counseling (1) | Personal Continuing Education (2) | Career Assistance (3) | Insurance | | Other (6) | | |
				Personal Medical (4)	Retirement (5)			
FROM DIOCESE, SYNOD, OR CONFERENCE:								
Catholic	$290	$303	$ 9	$366	$440	$ 19	$1,428	$1,039
Episcopalian	44	60	74	457	78	653	1,366	355
Lutheran	99	28	26	12	55	262	481	473
Methodist	57	57	58	1,162	2,104	231	3,670	297
FROM NATIONAL OFFICES:								
Catholic	--	--	--	--	--	--	--	--
Episcopalian	--	--	--	--	--	--	--	--
Lutheran	--	12	--	--	--	--	--	36
Methodist	--	21	--	--	--	--	--	286
TOTAL:								
Catholic	290	303	9	366	440	19	1,428	1,039
Episcopalian	44	60	74	457	78	653	1,366	355
Lutheran	99	40	26	12	55	262	481	509
Methodist	57	78	58	1,162	2,104	231	3,670	583

Table A.10

Catholic Religious Sisters: Average Total Compensation, Allowances, and Benefits, by Time Spent in Ministry, Parish Staffing Pattern, Region, and Type of Ministry

By Time, Parish Staffing, Region, & Ministry	Number	Total Compensation	Dollar Income	Housing/ Rent	Allowances*		Benefits*		
					Travel	Education	Retirement	Health	SECA/ WC
	(1)	(2)	(3)	(4)	(5)	(6)	(7)	(8)	(9)
ROMAN CATHOLIC SISTERS: BY TIME SPENT IN MINISTRY:									
Full-Time in Ministry	25	$15,120	$10,103	$2,315	$1,906	$419	$784	$1,103	$155
Part-Time in Ministry	11	9,975	6,564	2,348	2,077	360	375	594	–
FULL-TIME IN MINISTRY: BY PARISH STAFFING:									
Two or More Clergy	20	14,992	10,279	1,858	1,873	444	756	1,050	155
One Full-Time Clergy	3	15,959	9,724	4,296	–	250	975	1,569	–
No Full-Time Clergy	2	15,140	8,900	3,914	2,400	480	–	862	–
WESTERN STATES	7	17,135	13,891	637	1,083	326	1,047	1,059	77
NORTHEAST STATES	9	14,215	7,938	3,289	3,141	292	408	960	–
SOUTHEAST STATES	9	14,212	9,288	2,798	1,275	547	250	975	–

(Continued)

BY TYPE OF MINISTRY:

Christian Ed Director	9	15,238	10,679	1,829	1,929	365	807	1,237	—
Youth Director	2	16,095	14,699	—	100	259	1,080	864	—
Worship Director	1	22,470	7,170	13,300	1,500	—	—	500	—
Music Director	1	10,665	7,169	—	2,000	—	300	1,196	—
Organist	1	15,200	14,600	—	—	—	—	—	—
Administrative Assistant	—	—	—	—	—	—	—	—	—
Pastoral Associate	9	14,133	8,902	2,391	2,308	404	802	1,064	155
Other	1	16,572	9,000	3,300	1,700	—	750	1,172	—

*Unadjusted study data; allowances and benefits are for those receiving them. (See Table A.11)

Table A.11

Catholic Religious Sisters' Compensation Per Household, Housing, and Percent Receiving Allowances and Social Security: by Time Spent, Parish Staffing, Region and Type of Ministry

By Time Spent, Parish Staffing, Region & Ministry	Compensation Per Household	Housing* Utilities/Other	Housing* Comparable Rent	Unadjusted Percent Receiving						
				Allowances*				Benefits*		
				Utilities	Rent	Travel	Education	Retirement	Health	SECA/WC
	(1)	(2)	(3)	(4)	(5)	(6)	(7)	(8)	(9)	(10)
ROMAN CATHOLIC SISTERS:										
BY TIME SPEND IN MINISTRY:										
Full-Time in Ministry	$9	$3,054	$2,520	56%	24%	64%	56%	64%	64%	4%
Part-Time in Ministry	11	4,145	2,550	45	18	36	18	18	27	--
FULL-TIME IN MINISTRY:										
BY PARISH STAFFING:										
Two or More Clergy	8	3,229	2,700	45	15	75	55	65	65	5
One Full-Time Clergy	23	3,896	1,200	100	33	--	67	67	67	--
No Full-Time Clergy	1,081	1,004	2,910	100	100	50	50	50	50	--
WESTERN STATES	12	2,550	--	13	--	63	83	71	71	17
NORTHEAST STATES	7	4,636	2,400	73	57	67	33	53	43	--
SOUTHEAST STATES	370	2,058	970	93	33	43	50	60	60	--

(Continued)

BY TYPE OF MINISTRY:

Christian Ed. Director	9	3,053	1,200	56	11	56	56	78	67	--
Youth Director	11	--	--	--	--	50	100	50	50	--
Worship Director	8	9,400	3,900	100	100	100	--	--	100	--
Music Director	3	--	--	--	--	100	--	100	100	--
Organist	8	--	--	--	--	--	100	--	--	--
Administrative Assistant	--	--	--	--	--	--	--	--	--	--
Pastoral Associate	10	1,916	2,505	67	44	67	44	56	56	11
Other	9	3,300	--	100	--	100	100	100	100	--

* Unadjusted study data for those receiving allowances and/or benefits.

Table A.12

Full-Time Lay Professional Ministers: Total Compensation, Allowances, and Benefits (Excluding Catholic Religious Women), by Denomination and Parish Staffing Pattern

By Denomination & Parish Staffing	Number	Total Compensation	Dollar Income*	Housing/ Rent*	Allowances*		Benefits*		
					Travel	Education	Retirement	Health	SECA/ WC
	(1)	(2)	(3)	(4)	(5)	(6)	(7)	(8)	(9)
NATIONAL:									
Catholic	66	$19,818	$16,061	$ 293	$ 710	$495	$ 958	$1,255	$1,182
Episcopalian	31	16,754	13,532	442	1,256	348	1,457	1,984	991
Lutheran	17	19,463	15,978	745	1,563	487	1,805	1,005	1,273
Methodist	22	23,247	18,632	1,670	521	461	1,621	1,089	1,438
Average:	136	19,630	15,890	606	910	455	1,285	1,363	1,191
CATHOLIC:									
Two or More Clergy	50	19,823	15,918	387	726	376	922	1,255	1,148
One Full-Time Clergy	16	19,802	16,509	--	360	832	1,085	1,256	1,291
No Full-Time Clergy	--	--	--	--	--	--	--	--	--
EPISCOPAL:									
Two or More Clergy	22	18,168	14,519	623	1,672	284	1,883	2,074	1,045
One Full-Time Clergy	9	13,299	11,120	--	215	433	1,031	1,713	864
No Full-Time Clergy	--	--	--	--	--	--	--	--	--

(Continued)

LUTHERAN:									
Two or More Clergy	10	21,148	18,444	--	1,658	408	2,142	1,267	1,253
One Full-Time Clergy	7	17,056	12,455	1,809	1,475	553	--	743	1,259
No Full-Time Clergy	--	--	--	--	--	--	--	--	--
METHODIST:									
Two or More Clergy	19	23,579	18,982	1,618	650	526	1,621	1,105	1,362
One Full-Time Clergy	3	21,144	16,417	2,000	200	267	--	950	1,694
No Full-Time Clergy	--	--	--	--	--	--	--	--	--

* Unadjusted study data for those receiving allowances and/or benefits. (See Table A.13)

Table A.13

Full-Time Lay Professional Ministers: Compensation Per Household, Housing, and Percent Receiving Allowances and Benefits (Excluding Catholic Religious Women), by Time Spent, Parish Staffing, Region, and Type of Ministry

| By Denomination & Parish Staffing | Compensation Per Household | Housing* Utilities/Comparable | | Unadjusted Percent Receiving | | | | | | |
| | | | | Allowances + Utilities Rent Travel Education | | | | Benefits + Retirement Health SECA/WC | | |
	Household (1)	Other (2)	Rent (3)	Utilities (4)	Rent (5)	Travel (6)	Education (7)	Retirement (8)	Health (9)	SECA/WC (10)
NATIONAL:										
Catholic	$15	$1,965	$2,798	11%	30%	35%	64%	68%	85%	91%
Episcopalian	44	3,425	--	13	--	23	23	26	65	65
Lutheran	61	5,460	7,200	6	6	47	65	18	47	47
Methodist	24	7,011	8,700	18	5	32	55	45	86	59
BY DENOMINATION:										
CATHOLIC:										
Two or More Clergy	14	1,965	2,798	14	4	44	62	70	92	92
One Full-Time Clergy	21	--	--	--	--	6	69	63	63	88
No Full-Time Clergy	--	--	--	--	--	--	--	--	--	--
EPISCOPAL:										
Two or More Clergy	43	3,425	--	18	--	23	18	18	68	64
One Full-Time Clergy	48	--	--	--	--	22	33	44	56	67
No Full-Time Clergy	--	--	--	--	--	--	--	--	--	--

(Continued)

LUTHERAN:										
Two or More Clergy	56	—	—	16	5	40	50	20	40	40
One Full-Time Clergy	74	5,460	7,200	14	14	57	86	14	57	57
No Full-Time Clergy	—	—	—	—	—	—	—	—	—	—
METHODIST:										
Two or More Clergy	22	7,348	8,700	16	5	26	47	53	89	53
One Full-Time Clergy	65	6,000	—	33	—	67	100	—	67	100
No Full-Time Clergy	—	—	—	—	—	—	—	—	—	—

* Unadjusted study data for those receiving housing allowances.

+ Unadjusted study data showing percent receiving allowances and/or benefits.

Table A.14

Full-Time Lay Professional Ministers: Average Total Compensation, Allowances, and Benefits (Excluding Catholic Religious Women), by Region and Denomination

By Region & Denomination	Number	Total Compensation	Dollar Income	Housing/ Rent*	Allowances*		Benefits*		
					Travel	Education	Retirement	Health	SECA/ WC
	(1)	(2)	(3)	(4)	(5)	(6)	(7)	(8)	(9)
WESTERN STATES:									
Catholic	27	$21,601	$17,917	$	$ 330	$412	$1,110	$1,216	$1,262
Episcopalian	11	16,678	12,086	1,245	215	950	2,069	2,479	873
Lutheran	7	19,431	15,549	780	1,200	473	1,816	839	1,585
Methodist	8	26,163	23,310	750	1,200	750	1,463	1,828	--
Average	53	20,981	17,208	--	736	646	1,615	1,591	930
NORTHEAST STATES:									
Catholic	14	15,932	12,458	975	1,114	353	386	1,203	995
Episcopalian	5	16,827	14,554	--	120	--	204	1,062	840
Lutheran	2	26,692	16,650	3,600	1,100	--	777	1,651	--
Methodist	1	15,540	2,173	12,985	--	--	210	310	--
Average	22	17,096	12,848	7,140	584	353	394	1,057	918

(Continued)

SOUTHEAST STATES:

Catholic	25	20,068	16,075	34	1,111	730	957	1,276	1,169
Episcopalian	15	16,786	14,252	--	1,332	64	369	1,432	984
Lutheran	8	17,683	16,185	--	1,083	164	--	368	1,312
Methodist	13	23,934	19,014	1,838	267	406	675	1,148	1,148
Average	61	19,772	16,267	953	948	341	667	1,056	1,153

* Unadjusted study data showing averages for those receiving allowances and/or benefits. (See Table A.15)

Table A.15

Full-Time Lay Professional Ministers: Average Compensation Per Household, Housing, and Percent Receiving Allowances Social Security (Excluding Catholic Religious Women), by Denomination and Region

By Region & Denomination	Compensation Per Household (1)	Housing* Utilities/Comparable Other (2)	Housing* Rent (3)	Unadjusted Percent Receiving Allowances + Utilities (4)	Allowances + Rent (5)	Allowances + Travel (6)	Allowances + Education (7)	Benefits + Retirement (8)	Benefits + Health (9)	Benefits + SECA/WC (10)
WESTERN STATES:										
Catholic	16	--	--	--	--	45%	82%	70%	82%	95%
Episcopalian	17	$1,712	--	18%	--	9	9	14	45	--
Lutheran	73	2,730	--	17	--	46	100	29	54	54
Methodist	16	--	--	--	--	10	20	53	100	50
NORTHEAST STATES:										
Catholic	15	1,434	$1,088	19	5%	18	32	29	67	82
Episcopalian	55	--	--	--	--	33	--	33	22	67
Lutheran	33	--	2,400	--	33	67	67	33	33	--
Methodist	10	1,382	2,900	33	33	--	--	33	33	--
SOUTHEAST STATES:										
Catholic	16	760	1,140	17	3	23	67	79	94	95
Episcopalian	60	--	--	--	--	24	19	27	68	83
Lutheran	54	--	--	--	--	20	13	--	20	75
Methodist	44	2,656	--	20	--	56	81	28	70	80

* Unadjusted study data showing average allowance for those receiving.
+ Unadjusted study data showing percent of those receiving allowances and/or benefits.

Table A.16.1
Full-Time Lay Professional Ministers: Average Total Compensation, Allowances, and Benefits
(Excluding Catholic Religious Woman), by Type of Ministry

National Average By Type of Ministry	Number	Total Compensation	Dollar Income	Housing/ Rent*	Allowances* Travel	Education	Benefits* Retirement	Health	SECA/ WC
	(1)	(2)	(3)	(4)	(5)	(6)	(7)	(8)	(9)
NATIONAL AVERAGE:									
Christian Ed Director	30	$20,048	$16,146	$ 505	$ 862	$621	$1,144	$1,294	$1,163
Youth Director	18	20,925	16,593	1,091	607	362	838	1,195	1,313
Worship Director	4	19,887	16,631	--	200	350	1,059	1,006	1,181
Music Director	16	23,402	19,219	525	625	498	1,290	1,581	1,129
Organist	6	13,860	11,583	--	2,400	--	1,500	1,842	1,105
Administrative Assistant	34	19,668	16,745	17	1,051	426	1,275	1,434	1,168
Pastoral Associate	9	20,164	14,810	1,152	1,429	503	995	1,376	1,418
Other	16	16,862	12,880	1,582	680	314	1,301	1,005	1,068
Average:	133	19,814	16,055	--	913	440	1,176	1,338	1,184

* Unadjusted study data for those receiving allowances and/or benefits. (See Table A.16.2 below)

Table A.16.2

Full-Time Lay Professional Ministers: Average Compensation Per Household, Housing, and Percent Receiving Allowances and Social Security (Excluding Catholic Religious Women), by Denomination and Region

National Average By Type of Ministry	Compensation Per Household	Housing*		Unadjusted Percent Receiving *				Benefits +		
		Utilities/ Other	Comparable Rent	Allowances		Travel	Education	Retirement	Health	SECA/WC
				Utilities	Rent					
	(1)	(2)	(3)	(4)	(5)	(6)	(7)	(8)	(9)	(10)
NATIONAL AVERAGE:										
Christian Ed Director	$18	$3,910	$3,421	10%	33%	33%	70%	50%	70%	77%
Youth Director	20	3,644	8,700	17	6	39	83	61	94	78
Worship Director	14	--	--	--	--	25	50	75	100	100
Music Director	25	8,400	--	6	--	25	63	63	88	81
Organist	34	--	--	--	--	17	--	33	33	67
Administrative Assistant	25	588	--	3	--	24	29	41	71	76
Pastoral Associate	33	3,165	7,200	11	11	78	78	44	89	67
Other	16	4,629	2,175	31	6	38	44	44	69	69

* Unadusted study data for those receiving housing allowances

+ Unadjusted study data showing percent of those receiving allowances and/or benefits.

(Tables continue on the following page.)

Table A.17

Full-Time Lay Professional Ministers: Average Total Compensation, Allowances, and Benefits
(Excluding Catholic Religious Women), by Type of Ministry

By Denomination & Type of Ministry	Number Lay	Total Compen- sation	Dollar Income	Housing/ Rent*	Allowances*		Benefits*		
					Travel	Education	Retirement	Health	SECA/ WC
	(1)	(2)	(3)	(4)	(5)	(6)	(7)	(8)	(9)
CATHOLIC:									
Christian Ed Director	21	$18,782	$14,921	$ 269	$ 878	$689	$ 920	$1,220	$1,116
Youth Director	10	21,140	17,185	79	578	391	868	1,455	1,175
Worship Director	3	22,174	18,174	--	200	350	1,059	1,279	1,295
Music Director	7	19,270	16,265	--	--	390	702	1,110	1,118
Organist	1	4,220	4,220	--	--	--	--	--	--
Administrative Assistant	13	22,224	18,951	45	315	477	1,276	1,227	1,332
Pastoral Associate	4	21,201	15,660	791	1,301	432	995	1,484	1,247
Other	7	17,543	13,321	1,308	420	177	965	1,111	1,082
Average:	66	19,818	16,061						
EPISCOPALIAN:									
Christian Ed Director	1	11,572	10,800	--	--	--	--	--	722
Youth Director	1	27,245	21,600	--	960	--	--	2,691	1,544
Worship Director	--	--	--	--	--	--	--	--	--
Music Director	3	23,058	17,843	--	250	642	2,504	2,380	808
Organist	4	17,565	14,294	--	2,400	--	1,500	1,842	1,281

(Continued)

	N								
Administrative Assistant	14	16,880	14,116	--	1,295	100	912	1,984	991
Pastoral Associate	1	13,212	10,800	--	--	--	--	2,412	--
Other	5	13,207	10,055	2,140	--	175	--	1,129	661
Average:	29	17,028	13,855						
LUTHERAN:									
Christian Ed Director	4	23,615	19,665	--	1,400	505	2,142	3,302	1,260
Youth Director	2	19,598	17,890	--	--	200	--	925	1,164
Worship Director	--	--	--	--	--	--	--	--	--
Music Director	--	--	--	--	--	--	--	--	--
Organist	--	--	--	--	--	--	--	--	--
Administrative Assistant	4	16,946	15,519	--	2,200	200	--	112	782
Pastoral Associate	4	20,864	14,962	1,800	1,525	556	--	887	1,589
Other	2	18,555	13,600	2,730	2,000	--	--	--	1,430
Average:	16	20,126	16,473						
METHODIST:									
Christian Ed Director	4	25,246	20,397	2,375	200	400	--	1,047	1,759
Youth Director	5	19,762	13,890	3,769	400	417	755	536	1,960
Worship Director	1	13,027	12,000	--	--	--	--	187	840
Music Director	6	28,396	23,354	1,400	750	471	1,842	1,921	1,475
Organist	1	8,679	8,100	--	--	--	--	--	579
Administrative Assistant	3	25,234	21,093	--	--	--	--	1,357	1,455
Pastoral Associate	--	--	--	--	400	900	2,070	--	--
Other	2	21,926	17,684	--	--	--	--	--	--
Average	22	23,247	18,632	--	400	--	2,141	500	1,251

*Unadjusted study data for those receiving allowances and/or benefits

Table A.18

Full-Time Lay Professional Ministers' Average Compensation Per Household, Housing, and Percent Receiving Allowances and Benefits (Excluding Catholic Religious Women), by Denomination and Type of Ministry

	Compensation Per Household	Housing*		Unadjusted Percent Receiving						
		Utilities/	Comparable	Allowances*				Benefits*		
By Denomination & Type of Ministry		Other	Rent	Utilities	Rent*	Travel	Education	Retirement	Health	SECA/WC
	(1)	(2)	(3)	(4)	(5)	(6)	(7)	(8)	(9)	(10)
CATHOLIC:										
Christian Ed Director	$14	$1,114	$3,421	10%	5%	38%	71%	57%	81%	90%
Youth Director	16	786	-	10	-	50	100	80	90	100
Worship Director	15	-	-	-	-	33	67	100	100	100
Music Director	16	-	-	-	-	-	43	86	100	100
Organist	12	-	-	-	-	-	-	-	-	-
Administrative Assistant	18	588	-	8	-	15	46	54	77	92
Pastoral Associate	22	3,165	-	25	-	75	75	100	100	75
Other	10	3,492	2,175	29	14	57	43	71	86	86
EPISCOPALIAN:										
Christian Ed Director	38	-	-	-	-	-	-	-	-	100
Youth Director	115	-	-	-	-	100	100	-	100	100
Worship Director	-	-	-	-	-	-	-	-	-	-
Music Director	62	-	-	-	-	33	100	67	67	100
Organist	46	-	-	-	-	25	-	50	50	75

(Continued)

	(1)	(2)	(3)	(4)	(5)	(6)	(7)	(8)	(9)	(10)
Administrative Assistant	45	--	--	--	--	29	7	29	64	71
Pastoral Associate	24	--	--	--	--	--	--	--	100	--
Other	39	5,350	--	40	--	--	40	--	60	40
LUTHERAN:										
Christian Ed Director	48	--	--	--	--	25	75	50	25	25
Youth Director	67	--	--	--	--	--	50	--	100	50
Worship Director	--	--	--	--	--	--	--	--	--	--
Music Director	--	--	--	--	--	--	--	--	--	--
Organist	--	--	--	--	--	--	--	--	--	--
Administrative Assistant	67	--	--	--	--	25	50	25	50	50
Pastoral Associate	81	--	--	--	25	100	100	--	75	75
Other	89	5,460	7,200	50	--	50	50	--	--	50
METHODIST:										
Christian Ed Director	42	9,500	--	25	--	25	75	25	75	50
Youth Director	20	5,072	8,700	40	20	20	60	60	100	40
Worship Director	10	--	--	--	--	--	--	--	100	100
Music Director	30	8,400	--	17	--	50	67	33	83	50
Organist	15	--	--	--	--	--	--	--	--	100
Administrative Assistant	21	--	--	--	--	33	33	67	100	67
Pastoral Associate	--	--	--	--	--	--	--	--	--	--
Other	19	--	--	--	--	50	50	100	100	100

*Unadjusted study data for those receiving allowances and/or benefits.

Table A.19

Full-Time Lay Professional Ministers' Average Total Compensation, Allowances, and Benefits (Excluding Catholic Religious Women), by Region and Type of Ministry

By Region & Type of Ministry	Number	Total Compensation	Dollar Income	Housing/ Rent*	Allowances*		Benefits*		
					Travel	Education	Retirement	Health	SECA/ WC
	(1)	(2)	(3)	(4)	(5)	(6)	(7)	(8)	(9)
WESTERN STATES:									
Christian Ed Director	8	$20,059	$16,667	--	$ 203	$574	$1,476	$1,081	$1,124
Youth Director	8	19,218	16,529	--	252	338	960	917	1,086
Worship Director	3	9,942	8,333	--	100	175	567	457	590
Music Director	5	14,387	11,696	--	362	375	1,045	1,119	481
Organist	--	--	--	--	--	--	--	--	--
Administrative Assistant	15	21,173	17,751	--	210	495	1,344	1,783	1,298
Pastoral Associate	5	20,610	16,564	--	1,487	469	--	1,358	1,522
Other	7	18,302	12,783	$2,693	1,180	598	766	1,234	588
Average	51	18,916	15,443	--	482	464	1,019	1,277	1,040
NORTHEAST STATES:									
Christian Ed Director	8	14,212	11,915	65	617	318	322	1,035	775
Youth Director	2	11,813	5,625	4,544	--	--	--	739	415
Worship Director	--	--	--	--	--	--	--	--	--
Music Director	3	12,640	10,910	--	--	--	285	661	728
Organist	--	--	--	--	--	--	--	--	--

(Continued)

Administrative Assistant	6	16,468	14,226	--	200	--	--	1,007	1,002
Pastoral Associate	2	11,789	5,400	3,455	1,271	--	--	756	--
Other	1	3,770	800	2,970	--	--	--	--	--
Average	22	13,700	10,739	--	394	115	156	877	692
SOUTHEAST STATES:									
Christian Ed Director	14	22,079	17,791	723	1,493	509	330	1,217	1,362
Youth Director	8	23,119	19,006	667	504	256	332	1,251	1,370
Worship Director	1	6,632	5,508	--	--	--	--	428	394
Music Director	8	23,305	17,668	2,800	350	189	282	1,483	813
Organist	6	15,071	12,861	--	800	--	500	1,228	1,190
Administrative Assistant	13	18,911	16,363	98	867	317	342	855	1,097
Pastoral Associate	2	14,598	11,881	--	1,013	--	--	571	806
Other	8	11,136	9,492	42	333	72	276	610	686
Average	60	19,028	15,626	--	808	256	320	1,064	1,091

*Unadjusted study data for those receiving allowances and/or benefits. (See Table A.20)

Table A. 20

Full-Time Lay Professional Ministers' Average Compensation Per Household, Housing, and Percent Receiving Allowances and Benefits (Excluding Catholic Religious Women), by Region and Type of Ministry

By Region & Type of Ministry	Compensation Per Household	Housing*		Unadjusted Percent Receiving						
				Allowances +				Benefits +		
		Utilities/ Other	Comparable Rent	Utilities	Rent*	Travel	Education	Retirement	Health	SECA/WC
	(1)	(2)	(3)	(4)	(5)	(6)	(7)	(8)	(9)	(10)
WESTERN STATES:										
Christian Ed Director	$19	--	--	--	--	38%	88%	63%	75%	88%
Youth Director	16	--	--	--	--	38	88	50	88	75
Worship Director	8	--	--	--	--	17	33	33	50	50
Music Director	13	--	--	--	--	20	40	40	50	30
Organist	--	--	--	--	--	--	--	--	--	--
Administrative Assistant	22	--	--	--	--	19	36	61	83	69
Pastoral Associate	28	--	--	--	--	67	83	42	100	83
Other	31	$2,693	--	50%	--	54	54	50	67	50
NORTHEAST STATES:										
Christian Ed Director	17	262	--	8	--	28	36	25	36	81
Youth Director	10	1,644	$2,900	67	33%	--	33	67	67	33
Worship Director	--	--	--	►	►	►	--	--	--	--
Music Director	18	--	--	--	►		17	33	67	67
Organist	--	--	--	--	--	--	'	--	--	--

(Continued)

Administrative Assistant	33	–	–	–	–	17	–	17	67	83
Pastoral Associate	16	1,055	2,400	33	33	67	67	33	33	–
Other	2	2,245	725	33	33	–	–	–	–	–
SOUTHEAST STATES:									
Christian Ed Director	35	3,648	1,140	10	6	48	80	38	86	80
Youth Director	24	2,000	–	11	–	36	89	69	100	89
Worship Director	4	–	–	–	–	–	–	33	33	33
Music Director	34	2,800	–	33	–	23	80	37	77	67
Organist	46	–	–	–	–	11	–	22	44	72
Administrative Assistant	34	196	–	17	–	23	41	40	58	89
Pastoral Assistant	53	–	–	–	–	67	33	33	67	67
Other	11	83	–	17	–	22	17	28	56	61

* Unadjusted study data for those receiving housing allowances.

+ Unadjusted study data showing percet receiving allowances and/or benefits.

Table A. 21

Importance and Effectiveness on Twelve Leadership Tasks
(Percents)

Below are listed several leadership tasks in the parish/congregation. How important do you consider each of these to be? How effective is your current parish staff (ordained or lay) in carrying these out?

			Catholic	Episcopal	Lutheran	Methodist
1.	Preaching	Very important	87	81	91	92
		Quite effective	51	66	72	73
		Difference	36	15	19	19
2.	Planning or leading the Sunday liturgy or worship					
		Very important	83	79	78	73
		Quite effective	54	71	72	64
		Difference	29	8	6	9
3.	Parish visiting	Very important	42	50	58	63
		Quite effective	21	28	30	37
		Difference	21	22	28	26
4.	Pastoral counseling					
		Very important	64	68	72	64
		Quite effective	32	41	50	46
		Difference	32	27	22	18
5.	Directing religious education					
		Very important	82	66	72	70
		Quite effective	46	34	46	43
		Difference	36	32	26	27
6.	Directing social service ministries					
		Very important	42	22	32	26
		Quite effective	25	22	27	22
		Difference	17	0	5	4
7.	Hospital/ shut-in visiting	Very important	63	66	70	70
		Quite effective	42	49	58	65
		Difference	21	17	12	5

(Continued)

	Catholic	Episcopal	Lutheran	Methodist
8. Parish administration				
Very important	73	50	46	52
Quite effective	<u>50</u>	<u>41</u>	<u>42</u>	<u>47</u>
Difference	23	9	4	5
9. Deepening parishioners' spiritual lives				
Very important	87	81	78	82
Quite effective	<u>26</u>	<u>35</u>	<u>36</u>	<u>36</u>
Difference	61	46	42	46
10. Parish evangelization				
Very important	45	40	58	53
Quite effective	<u>12</u>	<u>19</u>	<u>21</u>	<u>18</u>
Difference	33	21	37	35
11. Long-range planning				
Very important	66	53	51	50
Quite effective	<u>24</u>	<u>25</u>	<u>23</u>	<u>33</u>
Difference	42	28	28	17
12. Leadership in the neighborhood or community				
Very important	44	34	34	39
Quite effective	<u>16</u>	<u>21</u>	<u>25</u>	<u>25</u>
Difference	28	13	9	14

Table A.22

Preference for Ordained Clergy or Lay Professional, by Parish Size (Percents)

	Catholic			Episcopal			Lutheran			Methodist		
	2+ F-T	1 F-T	0 F-T	2+ F-T	1 F-T	0 F-T	2+ F-T	1 F-T	0 F-T	2+ F-T	1 F-T	0 F-T
1. Preaching a sermon												
Ordained	47	57	63	71	74	88	88	76	85	86	82	83
Don't Care	49	40	30	29	26	11	12	24	15	13	18	15
Lay Person	3	4	7	1	0	1	0	1	0	1	0	2
2. Conducting a funeral												
Ordained	78	80	89	89	91	93	94	93	89	93	88	89
Don't Care	18	17	10	10	8	7	6	7	11	7	11	8
Lay Person	4	3	1	1	1	--	--	--	--	1	1	3
3. Counseling with you about a personal problem or decision												
Ordained	42	52	53	48	57	78	58	60	70	71	62	63
Don't Care	38	32	32	44	36	20	36	29	27	24	32	24
Lay Person	20	17	16	8	7	2	6	11	4	6	6	13
4. Leading a pastoral prayer												
Ordained	22	35	28	31	31	40	45	42	55	43	36	48
Don't Care	72	57	62	63	64	52	52	55	43	53	62	49
Lay Person	7	8	10	6	5	8	2	4	2	4	2	4

5. Reading the lessons in the worship service

Ordained	7	12	6	4	10	4	6	9	15	11	20
Don't Care	77	62	64	62	56	72	69	79	76	73	67
Lay Person	17	26	30	34	34	25	25	12	9	16	13

6. Visiting you in the hospital

Ordained	49	51	53	55	70	60	51	52	53	46	57
Don't Care	44	44	45	41	30	37	44	48	45	53	41
Lay Person	7	5	3	4	0	3	5	0	2	1	2

7. Managing the organizational affairs of the parish or congregation

Ordained	16	26	22	30	33	22	23	30	39	35	32
Don't Care	39	35	45	51	40	50	40	37	33	47	37
Lay Person	45	39	33	19	28	28	37	33	27	18	31

8. Teaching confirmation/new member classes

Ordained	20	28	58	61	67	57	60	77	61	62	70
Don't Care	56	39	33	30	26	39	33	20	32	32	24
Lay Person	24	33	9	9	7	4	7	4	7	6	7

9. Leading adult education classes or Bible study

Ordained	17	26	24	22	35	22	21	32	16	26	30
Don't Care	57	52	63	66	47	66	62	56	65	60	52
Lay Person	26	21	14	13	18	12	17	12	19	14	18

Lay Leader Questionnaire

This is the Protestant questionnaire. The Catholic version had slightly different wording, for example, "priests" instead of "ordained pastors," "parish" instead of "congregation or parish," and "parish council" instead of "governing board."

Questionnaire on Church Leadership

Dear Governing Board Member:

We invite your help in a nationwide study of professional leadership in congregations or parishes. Elected lay leaders in four denominations are being asked to tell us their attitudes through this questionnaire—Episcopal, Lutheran, Roman Catholic, and United Methodist. The purpose is to get comparative opinions that will help denominational leaders.

Recently there have been some changes in patterns in parish leadership, partly for financial reasons and partly for other reasons. While full-time, seminary-trained pastors and priests continue to be the most common form of parish leadership, there are other forms also. One is to have a priest or pastor serve several parishes. Another is to hire trained lay professionals (not ordained) to lead parishes. In some cases, ordained ministers can be hired part-time while they earn their main living elsewhere. We want your opinions about these arrangements.

In this questionnaire, the term lay professional means a non-ordained person paid for part-time or full-time ministry; the person is trained in college or seminary courses for Christian ministry.

Your parish may or may not have a full-time ordained pastor, and it may or may not have a lay professional. Some parishes have lay professionals in addition to full-time ordained pastors. In any event, we want your opinions about these alternative forms.

Would you take a few minutes to answer the following questions? Do not sign your name. Your responses will be seen only by the research team.

When you have finished, mail the questionnaire to us in the self-addressed envelope. Thank you.

> Dr. Jackson W. Carroll
> Hartford Seminary
>
> Dr. Dean R. Hoge
> Catholic University of America
>
> Rev. Francis K. Scheets, OSC
> Church Management Consultant

I. Parish Leadership

A. The following statements express various **attitudes about the roles and effectiveness of lay and ordained professional leadership.** Whether or not your congregation currrently employs a lay professional, please circle the number on the scale between 1 (strongly agree) and 4 (strongly disagree) that best reflects your opinion.

	AGREE		DISAGREE	
	Strongly	Somewhat	Somewhat	Strongly
1. Most of the tasks currently done by ordained pastors can be done equally well by lay persons with special competence for the task.	1	2	3	4
2. Paying trained lay persons to do tasks often done by ordained pastors is likely to undermine the prestige and authority of the pastor.	1	2	3	4
3. Paying trained lay persons to take responsibility for ministry tasks is likely to reduce the willingness of parishioners to volunteer their time to the congregation or parish.	1	2	3	4

B. Please indicate the extent to which you believe each of the following is true of **your congregation or parish:**

	Usually True	Somewhat True	Somewhat False	Usually False	Have No Opinion
1. The average lay person in this congregation/parish responds better to the leadership of someone who is ordained.	1	2	3	4	0
2. Our pastor seems to have more than enough time to accomplish the pastoral tasks required in this congregation or parish	1	2	3	4	0

	Usually True	Somewhat True	Somewhat False	Usually False	Have No Opinion
3. The pastor and lay leaders have difficulty in getting members to volunteer their time in helping with the ministry tasks of the congregation or parish.	1	2	3	4	0
4. If this congregation/ parish could not secure a full-time, professionally trained, ordained pastor, the members' morale would be adversely affected.	1	2	3	4	0
5. There is general satisfaction among the majority of the members with our current pattern of pastoral leadership.	1	2	3	4	0

C. If there were a decline in finances in your congregation/parish, or if a **full-time, seminary educated, ordained pastor were not available,** which of the following would you prefer your congregation/parish to employ to provide pastoral leadership? Please rank the choices from 1 (most prefer) to 4 (least prefer) in order of preference.

_____ an ordained, seminary-educated pastor who would work only part-time in your church while working part or full-time in another occupation.

_____ one or more lay members of the congregation/parish who are trained and authorized to fulfill most or all pastoral roles on a part-time basis.

_____ an ordained, seminary-educated pastor whom you would share with one or more other congregations/parishes

_____ a non-ordained person who has not had a formal seminary education, but has had training in pastoral leadership and is available to work full-time.

D. Please indicate below whether, given the choice, you would **prefer to have an ordained pastor or a trained lay professional** performing each of the listed activities. Or, indicate instead that it would make no difference to you.

	Prefer an Ordained Pastor	No Difference, Don't Care	Prefer a Trained Lay Person
1. Preaching a sermon	1	2	3
2. Conducting a funeral	1	2	3
3. Counseling with you about a personal problem or decision	1	2	3
4. Leading a pastoral prayer	1	2	3
5. Reading the lessons in the worship service	1	2	3
6. Visiting you in the hospital	1	2	3
7. Managing the organizational affairs of the parish or congregation	1	2	3
8. Teaching confirmation/new member classes	1	2	3
9. Leading adult education classes or Bible study	1	2	3

E. How do you feel about the use in parish or congregational leadership of **"tent-making" ministers** (that is, ordained or lay professional ministers whose principle income derives from non-church sources)? Circle one number:

1. An exciting development
2. Should be encouraged in some cases but not generally
3. Appropriate for lay professionals but not for ordained persons
4. A regrettable but financially necessary development
5. A regrettable development that should be stopped

II. Characteristics of Your Congregation or Parish and Its Current Leadership

A. What is the name and address of your parish/congregation? _____

_____

B. What is the denominational affiliation of the parish/congregation?

(1) ____ Catholic (2) ____ Episcopal (3) ____ Lutheran (4) ____ United Methodist

C. Would you say that the financial health of the parish/congregation is:

(1) ____ excellent   (4) ____ in some difficulty

(2) ____ good   (5) ____ in serious difficulty

(3) ____ tight but adequate

D. The current morale of the members is:

(1) ____ high   (3) ____ moderately low

(2) ____ moderately high   (4) ____ low

E. Which of the following best describes lay involvement in your congregation/parish? (Check one)

(1) ____   There are a few active lay people, but most of the parishioners are Sunday-morning only.

(2) ____   There are several committees/boards in the congregation/parish that are active, but only a relatively small percentage of the members are involved other than on Sunday.

(3) ____   There is an active majority of the members who are involved in boards and committees, worship, study and outreach programs of the congregation/parish.

F. Important decisions about the life of the congregation/parish are rarely made without open discussion by church leaders and members.

(1) ____ agree   (3) ____ moderately disagree

(2) ____ moderately agree   (4) ____ disagree

G. How much "say" or influence do you think that each of the following persons or groups has in determining the policies and programs of this congregation/parish? Circle one number on each line.

	Very Great	Great	Some	Little	None
The pastor	1	2	3	4	5
Other staff (skip if none)	1	2	3	4	5
Governing board/parish council	1	2	3	4	5
A majority of the church membership (excluding the governing board)	1	2	3	4	5
One or more powerful individuals in the congregation/parish	1	2	3	4	5
The diocese/synod/ conference	1	2	3	4	5
Yourself	1	2	3	4	5

H. How much "say" or influence do you think that each of the following ought to have in determining the policies and programs of this congregation/parish? Circle one number on each line.

	Very Great	Great	Some	Little	None
The pastor	1	2	3	4	5
Other staff (skip if none)	1	2	3	4	5
Governing board/parish council	1	2	3	4	5
A majority of the church membership (excluding the governing board)	1	2	3	4	5
One or more powerful individuals in the congregation/parish	1	2	3	4	5
The diocese/synod/ conference	1	2	3	4	5
Yourself	1	2	3	4	5

I. This section is concerned with two questions. Below are listed several **leadership tasks** in the parish/congregation. First, **how important** do you consider each of these to be? (Circle a number in the first 3 columns).

Second, **how effective** is **your current parish staff** (ordained or lay) in carrying these out? (Circle a number in the 4 columns to the right. If no staff person is doing the task, circle 0.)

	IMPORTANCE			EFFECTIVENESS			
	Very	Moderate	Not Very	Quite	Somewhat	Not Very	No Staff
1. Preaching	1	2	3	1	2	3	0
2. Planning or leading the Sunday liturgy or worship	1	2	3	1	2	3	0
3. Parish visiting	1	2	3	1	2	3	0
4. Pastoral counseling	1	2	3	1	2	3	0
5. Directing religious education	1	2	3	1	2	3	0
6. Directing social service ministries	1	2	3	1	2	3	0
7. Hospital/shut-in visiting	1	2	3	1	2	3	0
8. Parish administration	1	2	3	1	2	3	0
9. Deepening parishioners' spiritual lives	1	2	3	1	2	3	0
10. Parish evangelization	1	2	3	1	2	3	0
11. Long-range parish planning	1	2	3	1	2	3	0
12. Leadership in the neighborhood or community	1	2	3	1	2	3	0

III. Some Information About Yourself

A. Have you ever been a member of a denomination other than this one?

   (1) _____ yes   (2) _____ no   (if yes, which was the denomination during your upbringing?)

_____

B. What is your sex? (1) _____ female (2) _____ male

C. What is your highest level of education? (Check one)

   (1) _____ High school graduation or less

   (2) _____ Some college or technical training

   (3) _____ College graduate

   (4) _____ Post college (graduate or professional)

THANK YOU VERY MUCH FOR YOUR PARTICIPATION IN COMPLETING THIS QUESTIONNAIRE. PLEASE PUT YOUR COMPLETED QUESTIONNAIRE IN THE ATTACHED, SELF-ADDRESSED ENVELOPE (No Postage Required), and DROP IT IN THE MAIL.

Center for Social and Religious Research
Hartford Seminary
77 Sherman Street
Hartford, Connecticut 06105

We welcome any comments you wish to add.

Notes

Introduction

1. Perhaps the most important indication of converence among Protestants has been the ecumenical document *Baptism, Eucharist, and Ministry* (World Council of Churches, 1982), which points to major agreement about ministry in various denominations. Roman Catholics were observers in the development of the document. The Catholic theologian Schillebeeckx comments favorably on this document in *The Church With a Human Face* (1985).

Chapter 1

1. We use the word "parish" to describe local churches in both Catholic and Protestant traditions. Also we use the term "clergy" to denote ordained ministers, both Protestant and Catholic.

2. There is some ambiguity regarding the number of Catholics in the U.S. *The Official Catholic Directory* lists fewer members than there are individuals who state a Catholic preference in public opinion polls. The same is true for Protestants when official membership numbers and poll data on religious preference are compared.

3. The figures we used for the Protestant ratios come from the *Yearbook of American and Canadian Churches* (1987) and the *General Minutes of the United Methodist Church* (1986). They are based on inclusive membership and total number of clergy, including retired clergy.

4. Lutheran and Episcopal figures come from the *Yearbook of American and Canadian Churches* and include both active and

retired clergy. The United Methodist figures come from United Methodist *General Minutes* and do not include retired clergy. If we are correct in assuming that the number of retirements has increased, the Episcopal and Lutheran figures probably slightly overrepresent the increases of the past 10 years in comparison with the Methodist figures.

5. The 1965 figures include both Methodists and Evangelical United Brethren. The two united in 1968 to form the United Methodist Church.

6. The sources for these calculations are Carroll, Marty and Johnson (1979:23) and the *Yearbook for American and Canadian Churches,* 1987. The dramatic increase in Episcopal contributions, according to an Episcopal Church official, is a result of a major funding campaign, Venture in Mission, and general efforts to increase the financial stewardship of members.

7. The vacancies also reflected the location of many of the vacant churches: often in small towns and rural areas some distance from major population centers.

8. For a summary of both positive and negative aspects of the permanent diaconate see, for example, discussions by Joseph Komonchak (1985), Paul Hypher (1985), and Philip Murnion (1985).

9. The Communion Service was approved by the Vatican in the 1980's for use in worshipping communities not having a priest present. The service resembled the Mass except that there is no Eucharist prayer of consecration and the worshippers are served communion elements consecrated earlier by a priest.

Chapter 3

1. Some judicatories require that parishes providing housing to clergy pay a percentage of the clergy's salary into an equity fund. This is intended to provide "housing equity" at the time of retirement. See Holck (1985).

2. The concept "Net Assignable Square Footage" was first developed by Fred Putney of the Riverside Group, Fort Lee, NJ, for a Columbia University study of medical library costs.

3. The adjustment calculations were done to provide the best estimate of overall compensation figures in each denomination. Since our sample overrepresented large parishes, these had to be down-weighted in an overall estimate. For example, the total compensation of Catholic priests was $25,041 in parishes with two or more full-time priests, $28,201 in parishes with one priest, and $19,464 in parishes with less than a full-time priest. The adjusted overall figure was (.50 x 25,041) + (.45 x 28,201) + (.05 x 19, 464) = 26,184.

4. An earlier version of Table 3.4 was published in the 1988 *Yearbook of American and Canadian Churches,* and it had a higher figure for Episcopalian clergy—$45,005 rather than $41,029. The $41,029 here is more defensible. The difference occurred because of lack of precise data available for the adjustment formula in the Episcopal Church. At first we were given one set of estimates of Episcopal parish size, then we checked and were given a second set. All unadjusted data are unaffected by this problem.

5. During the research process we had difficulty achieving uniformity in definitions at this point, so the "other" expenditures are not exactly comparable from denomination to denomination. The figures must be seen as approximations.

6. The total costs of seminary education are much higher. The true annual costs in 1986-87 per full-time-equivalent student were $11,442 for Catholic seminaries, $20,399 for Episcopalian, $10,775 for Lutheran, and $12,062 for Methodist, according to the *Fact Book on Theological Education, 1987-88* (Baumgaertner, 1988).

Chapter 4

1. As an approximate check on our findings, we can compare these compensation levels with the 1986 survey of the National Association of Church Business Administrators. That survey has methodological flaws, but we may mention some of its findings regarding lay professional compensations. In our study we found an average of $20,048 for Christian Education Directors, and they found $16,806. For Youth Directors we found $20,925 and the found $27,814. For Music Directors we found $23,402 and they found $24,176. For Administrative Assistants we found $19,668 and they found $14,024. The differences may be due to sampling problems or noncomparable definitions.

Chapter 5

1. For simplicity we use the term "clergy" to include all ordained and trained ministers and priests. Also we use the word "parish" to include parishes and congregations.

Our analysis uses percent difference as a criterion of strength of relationships, not traditional significance tests. This is done for clarity of exposition. Ordinarily we use a 12-point percentage spread as minimal for mention in the text. Tables with 12-point spreads (when comparing staffing levels within a single denomination) typically have a significance level of about .07 if the percentages are near 0 or 100, or about .12 if the percentages are near 50. Tables comparing the four denominations (when N is about 1800) with a 12-point spread are all significant beyond .01. To avoid erroneous conclusions, in the text we emphasize percentage differences of 14 points or more, especially when they occur in several related tables.

Chapter 6

1. Data for secondary school teachers and college professors is from the *Statistical Abstract of the United States, 1986* (U.S. Census, 1986). Social work salary data came from the National Association of Social Workers.

2. For a discussion of the strengths and limitations of dual-role clergy, see Carroll and Wilson (1980:131ff). For a similar discussion of use of indigenous lay ministers, see Tiller (1983: 123ff).

References

Baumgaertner, William L. (ed.) 1988. *Fact Book on Theological Education, 1987-88.* Vandalia, OH: Association of Theological Schools.

Bonn, Robert L. 1974. *Clergy Support Study—1973.* New York: Professional Church Leadership, National Council of Churches.

_____. 1975. "Moonlighting Clergy." *The Christian Ministry,* (September): 4-8.

Broccolo, Gerald T. 1986. "Can We Have Prayer Without Father?" *Journal of the Catholic Campus Ministry Association* 1 (Spring): 22-24.

Carroll, Jackson W. (ed.) 1977. *Small Churches are Beautiful.* San Francisco: Harper and Row.

Carroll, Jackson W., and David A. Roozen. 1984. "Trends in Seminary Enrollments and Finances: Comparison of Mainline Protestants, Evangelical Protestants, and Roman Catholics." Unpublished paper presented at the Meeting of the Religious Research Association, Chicago, IL.

Carroll, Jackson W., and Robert L. Wilson. 1980. *Too Many Pastors? The Clergy Job Market.* New York: Pilgrim Press.

Carroll, Jackson W., Barbara Hargrove, and Adair T. Lummis. 1983. *Women of the Cloth.* San Francisco: Harper and Row.

Carroll, Jackson W., Martin E. Marty, and Douglas W. Johnson. 1979. *Religion in America, 1950 to the Present.* San Francisco: Harper and Row.

Census, U. S. Bureau of. 1986. *Statistical Abstract of the United States: 1986.* Washington, D.C.: U.S. Government Printing Office.

Diocese of Pittsburgh. 1978. *Priests' Compensation Study.* Pittsburgh, PA: Diocesan Office for Research and Planning.

_____. 1981. *Clergy Expense Allowance Study.* Pittsburgh, PA: Diocesan Office for Research and Planning.

Diocese of Richmond. 1976. *Report of the Task Force on Salaries/Stipends.* Mimeographed report. Diocese of Richmond, VA.

Dudley, Carl S. 1978. *Making the Small Church Effective.* Nashville: Abingdon Press.

Elsesser, Suzanne E. 1983. "Priestless Parishes: A New Look at How They Are Being Staffed." Research report. Cincinnati, OH: National Association of Church Personnel Administrators.

_____. 1986. "Parishes Without Resident Priests." Photocopied paper. New York: National Pastoral Life Center.

Frensdorff, Wesley, and Charles R. Wilson. 1987. *Challenge for Change: Clergy and Congregations.* Arvada, CO: Jethro Publications.

Gilmour, Peter. 1986. *The Emerging Pastor: Non-Ordained Catholic Pastors.* Kansas City: Sheed and Ward.

Gallup, George, Jr., and Jim Castelli. 1987. *The American Catholic People: Their Beliefs, Practices, and Values.* Garden City, NY: Doubleday.

Greeley, Andrew M. 1972. *The Catholic Priest in the United States: Sociological Investigations.* Washington: United States Catholic Conference.

Greeley, Andrew M., and William E. McManus. 1987. *Catholic Contributions: Sociology and Policy.* Chicago: Thomas More Press.

Hartley, Loyde H. 1984. *Understanding Church Finances: The Economics of the Local Church.* New York: Pilgrim Press.

Hemrick, Eugene F., and Dean R. Hoge. 1985. *Seminarians in Theology: A National Profile.* Washington: United States Catholic Conference.

_____. 1987. *Seminary Life and Visions of the Priesthood: A National Survey of Seminarians.* Washington: National Catholic Educational Association.

Hoge, Dean R. 1987. *The Future of Catholic Leadership: Responses to the Priest Shortage.* Kansas City: Sheed and Ward.

Hoge, Dean R., Raymond H. Potvin, and Kathleen M. Ferry. 1984. *Research on Men's Vocations to the Priesthood and Religious Life.* Washington: United States Catholic Conference.

Holck, Manfred, Jr. 1985. *Clergy Desk Book.* Nashville, TN: Abingdon Press.

Hypher, Paul H. 1985. "The Restoring of the Diaconate." Pp. 39-46 in *The Diaconal Reader*. Washington: United States Catholic Conference.

Jacquet, Constant (ed.). 1986. *Yearbook of American and Canadian Churches*. Annual. Nashville, TN: Abingdon Press.

Judy, Martin T. 1973. *The Parish Development Process*. Nashville, TN: Abingdon Press.

Komonchak, Joseph A. 1985. "The Permanent Diaconate and the Variety of Ministries in the Church." Pp. 12-38 in *The Diaconal Reader*. Washington: United States Catholic Conference.

Mathieson, Moira. 1979. *The Shepherds of the Delectable Mountains*. Cincinnati, OH: Forward Movement Publications.

Murnion, Philip J. 1985. "The Diaconate in the Context of Today's Ministry." Pp. 65-77 in *The Diaconal Reader*. Washington: United States Catholic Conference.

NACBA & MSFA. 1986. *National Church Staff Salary Survey: 1986*. Lubbock, TX: Ministers Financial Service Association.

NATRI. 1985. *Arch/Diocesan Compensation Survey*. Silver Spring, MD: National Association of Treasurers of Religious Institutes.

_____. 1987. *Arch/Diocesan Compensation Survey*. Silver Spring, MD: National Association of Treasurers of Religious Institutes.

NFPC. 1984. *The Laborer is Worthy of His Hire: A Survey of Salary and Benefits Paid to Priests by the Dioceses of the U.S.* Booklet. Chicago: National Federation of Priests' Councils.

Parish Project. 1982. *Parish Life in the United States: Final Report to the Bishops.* Washington: United States Catholic Conference.

Roozen, David A., and Adair T. Lummis. 1987. "Leadership and Theological Education in the Episcopal Church." Report. Hartford, CT: Hartford Seminary Center for Social and Religious Research.

Rothage, Arlin J., n.d. "Sizing Up a Congregation for a New Member Ministry." Report. New York: Episcopal Church Center.

Russell, Anthony. 1980. *The Clergy Profession.* London: S.P.C.K. Publications.

Schaller, Lyle E. 1982. *Small Churches are Different.* Nashville, TN: Abingdon Press.

_____. 1985. *The Mid-Sized Church.* Nashville, TN: Abingdon Press.

_____. 1987. "UMC: What's the Future of the Small-Church Denomination?" *Circuit Rider* 11 (December-January): 8-10.

Scheets, Francis Kelly, OSC. 1981. "Will There Be Seminarians in 1990?" *The Priest* 37:11, pp. 10-13.

_____. 1982. "The American Catholic Church--Alive and Well?" *The Priest* 38:10, pp. 40-45.

_____. 1985. *NCEA Update of the CARA/Lilly Study, 1980-1984: Training Manual.* Washington: National Catholic Educational Association Seminary Department.

_____. 1987. "Another Neighborhood Parish Abandoned." *The Priest* 43:1, pp. 35-42.

Schillebeeckx, Edward. 1985. *The Church With a Human Face.* New York: Crossroad.

Schoenherr, Richard, and Annemette Sorensen. 1982. "Social Change in Religious Organizations: Consequences of Clergy Decline in the U.S. Catholic Church." *Sociological Analysis* 43 (Spring): 23-52.

Sherry, Robert. 1985. "Shortage? What Vocation Shortage?" *The Priest* 41 (November): 29-32.

Tiller, John. 1983. *A Strategy for the Church's Ministry.* London: CIO Publishers.

Wall Street Journal. 1986. "U.S. Sisters in Need: U.S. Nuns Face Crisis," by John Fialka, May 19, p. l.

_____. 1988. "Housing Expenses" (article). February 12, p. 17.

Walrath, Douglas Alan (ed.). 1983. *New Possibilities for Small Churches.* New York: Pilgrim Press.

Wilson, Charles R. 1988. "St. Swithen's Swamped: The Story of a Pastoral Church." *Interchange* 6 (Winter): 2-4.

World Council of Churches. 1982. *Baptism, Eucharist, and Ministry.* Geneva: World Council of Churches.